A

GRIEF ALLY

HELPING PEOPLE YOU LOVE
COPE WITH
DEATH, LOSS, AND GRIEF

Copyright © 2022 Alyssa Bird

All rights reserved. No part of this publication may be reproduced, distributed, or transmitted in any form or by any means, including photocopying, recording, or other electronic or mechanical methods, without the prior written permission of the publisher, except in the case of brief quotations embodied in critical reviews and certain other noncommercial uses permitted by copyright law. For permission requests, write to the publisher, addressed "Attention: Permissions Coordinator," at the address below.

Bittersweet
Tooth
Publishing

Contact information for Bittersweet Tooth Publishing
hello@bittersweettoothpublishing.com

ISBN: 978-1-7386528-2-2 (paperback)
ISBN: 978-1-7386528-1-5 (ebook)
ISBN: 978-1-7386528-3-9 (audiobook)

Ordering Information:
Special discounts are available on quantity purchases by corporations, associations, and others. For details, contact hello@bittersweettoothpublishing.com

I wrote this book as a guest on the traditional unceded territory of the K'ómoks First Nation.

To Will, my beloved.
Thank you for always believing in my wildest dreams even when you didn't want to.

TABLE OF CONTENTS

Chapter 1	After the Worst Has Happened, What Happens Now?	1
Chapter 2	You Can't Fix This: What You Need to Know about Grief to Be an Ally	11
Chapter 3	You Can't Take Care of Your Person If You Aren't Caring for Yourself	23
Chapter 4	Allies, Not Enemies: How to Be Part of Your Person's Support Team	41
Chapter 5	Listening without Fixing: The One Skill You Need to Have	55
Chapter 6	Poetry, Clichés, and Nonsense: What Not to Say	71
Chapter 7	You're Going to Make Mistakes: This Is How to Recover	89
Chapter 8	The Long Haul and Beyond	103
Chapter 9	Welcome to the Grief Revolution	113

AUTHOR'S NOTE

Dear Reader,

Thank you for being here. Thank you for being willing to learn how to be the best source of support for someone whom you love who is grieving. With that being said, I want you to know that it is also very important for you to take care of yourself in your role as a grief ally.

Grief allyship is a challenging role, and it requires a lot of energy to do it well. If you are also hurting because of this death in your community, this is your permission slip to take a moment and reflect on whether you're capable of doing this job right now. If you are drowning on your own, it is okay to find a life vest or swim to the shallow end of the pool where you can stand before offering help to someone else. That act is not selfish. It's how you'll survive.

The lessons here will still apply when you're more resourced and capable of soaking up what you are learning. I will also be here to support you as well.

Until you are ready, I wish you ease in taking care of yourself.

With love,

Aly

CHAPTER 1

AFTER THE WORST HAS HAPPENED, WHAT HAPPENS NOW?

Someone Died

If you're here, reading Chapter 1, I'm really sorry. I know what that means.

Someone died.

Death is significant and confusing and earth-shattering and life-changing for anyone, and especially when it happens to one of the most important people in your life, one whom you love with your whole heart. You care about each other so deeply that your relationship can't even be defined. Whether they're your best friend, lover, sister, brother, neighbor, personal trainer, dog walker, former employee, or coworker, they are *your* person. Now, your person's beloved is dead, and you need to know what to do next.

I know you're willing to do anything for your person—*literally* anything. You're on the hunt for answers to questions like:

"What do I do?!"
"How do I help?!"
"What do I say?!"
"What's the right thing to do right now?!"
"How do I not screw this up?!"
"Can I do this if I don't know what I'm doing?!"
"What do I do if I live far away?!"
"Is my person going to be able to survive this?!"
"Why does every resource tell me to bring food?!"

I also know you're ready to charge into battle for your person if only someone would give you a horse and sword and point you in the right direction, like *Game of Thrones'* Robb Stark, but I need you to pause for a second. This isn't the moment for a battle. Grief isn't a villain or an enemy. It is simply the bittersweet consequence of being a human capable of loving others. There isn't a cure for grief. There is nothing that you can do to take away another's or your own grief. There's nothing that you or anyone else can do to change the devastating reality that as humans we all die one day, some of us too soon, without enough warning, and some not peacefully. But even though you can't conquer grief like territory to be won, you have power here to alleviate sorrow.

Over and over, studies have shown that the quality of someone's social support network is a powerful indicator of how well they'll be able to cope, grow, and recover from traumatic life experiences.[1] What that means for you is how your person is supported in their grief. The way that you and others who show up to help will impact whether your person can reach a different but capable—*kind of okay*—footing after the worst has happened. Whether your person's beloved is their life partner, significant other, child, parent, or someone whose relationship or role is less easily defined, you have power…you can help.

If you're willing to commit to a few hours of reading, I can teach you how to offer the kind of social support that your person needs. It will take time and will not be easy, but if you love your person as much as I think you do (because you picked up this book), I know that you are more than capable of learning how to be a grief ally.

The Reality of Loss

Pop culture moments might have prepared you for the shock of death, but the plot lines from *Grey's Anatomy, Sex in the City,* or *New Amsterdam* are missing the details about what to do now—after the flowers have been sent, and the lasagnas have been dropped off, and the rituals have been held. What do you do after that? Because death changes everything, you know that you have to do more for your person.

Your person will need you in their future more than they ever did before. They'll need people who are willing to step up and to stand down when they're asked to. They'll need people in their life who are willing to truly see and feel what they're experiencing and to be accepted in whatever state they are in. They'll need people to love them as they shift and change and grow into a future without their beloved. Your person is going to need you to be a grief ally.

Showing up for someone living with grief is excruciatingly uncomfortable, probably messier than anything you've ever experienced, and wildly unpredictable. But you love your person no matter what, right? Such moments and all the unpredictability that lies ahead is when you get to put the *no matter what* into practice.

So, after all the ceremonies, customs, and formalities, you

have to continue supporting your person with unconditional love, understanding, empowerment, and respect. Such support requires specific skills and a mindset that take practice to master, but once obtained, they become a framework that will help you navigate nearly every situation involving your person and their grief in this post-loss life.

Learning how to be a grief ally in the short term is going to give you a place to focus your energy. All the empathy, anxiety, and discomfort that's built up in your body over the loss can be channeled into learning what will be helpful to your person as more time passes. It's going to give you the confidence to know that you're being helpful instead of harmful. Ultimately, learning how to be a grief ally is going to give you the courage that you'll need to keep showing up even when you make mistakes. That's the kind of courage that would make Brené Brown, the renowned vulnerability researcher, proud and is the kind of courage that your person is going to need from you as they learn how to live with their circumstances. It's not going to be easy, but it will set you up for success. I can give you this assurance with certainty because I've lived it.

I Know Grief, Intimately

On an average day in November, my husband,[*] Will, woke up, told me he loved me, kissed me goodbye, and then never came home alive. I became a widow at 30 years old, instantly, unintentionally,

---

[*] For those who are sticklers on definitions, technically, when Will died, he was not my husband. Although we had been in a common-law relationship since 2015, we never had the chance to stand in front of witnesses and be declared husband and wife, despite talking openly about doing so in our future. So, for the sake of simplicity and how I feel in my heart, I've adopted the labels husband and wife, and I apply them liberally.

and without any experience or knowledge about what living with a devastating loss looks like. To say that I was thrown into the deep end would be an understatement. But what has kept me from drowning has been the way my community has courageously showed up to help me survive. That's what your person needs from you. Unfortunately, though, courage is the exception, not the rule.

In the early days after Will died, a grief expert suggested I find *community*. "Go find people like you because you're now living with something very different than that of your peers" was what they said. So, I tried. I joined 13 different Facebook groups for widows, but before I started sharing my experience, I listened to the stories of others. I very quickly realized that the support I was receiving from the people who love me the most was very different from how my widowed peers were experiencing grief.

They described feeling abandoned, forgotten, or shamed for not being able to move on. My community, on the other hand, has never treated me and my grief with intolerance or apathy. They have bravely remained by my side since the day my life was shattered. Despite being afraid, making mistakes, and having to face their own grief for the loss of the one who was loved by me, they've tended to my heart and my needs. It's my goal to teach you how to provide that same level of devotion to your person as they grieve the death of their beloved or another, so that everyone–your person included–is able to receive the kind of support needed to cope with life-changing loss.

Since Will's death, I've poured my heart into synthesizing the lessons that someone like you needs to know to provide the best support possible for your person. I've studied grief psychology, biology, and culture. I have fused what you need to know with my decade of community development and life-coaching experience. With this book, you'll be able to climb up the learning curve of grief support faster than has ever been possible.

About This Book

What I have to teach you in this book is rooted in the death of a partner or spouse because that is where my experience lies, but my lessons are universal. If your person has experienced the death of someone who was significant in their life, this book is going to be extremely helpful to you—regardless of what kind of relationship your person had with their beloved.

This book is meant to be read from the beginning to end. The lessons in each chapter build on one another, with the foundational stuff up front. This is the kind of book in which you should feel free to tag pages, highlight what is meaningful to you, and make notes in the margins. This book is *your* guide.

Here's what you can expect to learn from each chapter:

- ***Chapter 2: You Can't Fix This: What You Need to Know about Grief to Be an Ally***

  Up front, I offer a quick and easy overview of exactly what you need to know about grief to be a grief ally.

- ***Chapter 3: You Can't Take Care of Your Person If You Aren't Caring for Yourself***

  Here I'll teach you how to take care of yourself—and why—as you support your person.

- ***Chapter 4: Allies, Not Enemies: How to Be Part of Your Person's Support Team***

  Next up, you'll learn why you need to empower your person to be the leader and the expert of their own grief. We'll also cover the mindset you need in order to work with others who want to help too.

- **Chapter 5: Listening without Fixing: The One Skill You Need to Have**

    We'll take a deep dive into the single most important skill that every grief ally needs: the ability to actively listen.

- **Chapter 6: Poetry, Clichés, and Nonsense: What Not to Say**

    Here I'll give you some guidance on what to not say to someone whose beloved has died.

- **Chapter 7: You're Going to Make Mistakes; This Is How to Recover**

    Mistakes are a big part of how we learn. In this chapter, we'll go over how to recover and apologize to your person when you make a mistake.

- **Chapter 8: The Long Haul and Beyond**

    This chapter is about how to remain a grief ally as time moves forward and more life happens. It offers the lessons to which you need to adhere so that your person remains your person through the rest of life's ups and downs.

- **Chapter 9: Welcome to the Grief Revolution**

    And finally, we'll stand back and take a "big picture" look at everything we've learned and why grief allyship is so important. Here, I offer you my personal thanks for being willing to be there for your person and explain why everyone who is bereaved needs allyship like yours through the long haul of grief. I also offer some ideas for additional resources you can utilize as you move forward, putting what you've learned into practice as a grief ally.

Each chapter begins with a guiding promise. Consider them to be promises that you're making to your person. Your goal in supporting your person through the long haul of their grief should be to keep those promises. If you can do that, you're doing the *right* thing. Similarly, each chapter ends with examples of what grief allyship in action looks like. Use the examples as inspiration, and brainstorm your own as well.

If you find, once you finish reading, that you want to continue to learn more about grief and loss, I've included a list of additional resources at the end of the book for you to explore.

You Can Be a Grief Ally

In her book *Grief Works*, Julia Samuel wrote:

> "Grieving is lonely-making. All that missing, and wanting, and not finding can feel like excruciating loneliness. Warm, caring, human contact helps take the chill out of it. It can't make the pain go away, but being connected and remembered helps your friend to bear it."[2]

Julia couldn't be more right. Your person needs *you*. They need your unconditional love, your courage, and your reverence for what they're experiencing because their beloved is gone. And showing up and giving that support to them is how your person gets to remain your person.

In *Grey's Anatomy*, Meredith and Cristina didn't become each other's person because they were enduring happiness. The strength of their "person-ship" was determined by being there for one another through the shittiest things that happen in life, including death. And the irony in being able to show up for your person in the worst of times means that you'll be there for each other through the really amazing things too—weddings, babies, career milestones, lifetime achievements, etc. That's what you're going to be able to do by reading this book.

By learning how to be the best source of support for your person, you're equipping yourself with the tools that you need to navigate the immediate shock, anxiety, and chaos after someone dies. But you're also building a foundation that you can rely on for the rest of your person-ship—not to mention when you inevitably lose someone who is beloved by you—to get the support that you deserve.

Being a grief ally is a difficult task. It's not something that any of us wishes for, but it's one of the most important roles we can ever embody.

So, with that, are you ready to be a grief ally?

CHAPTER 2

YOU CAN'T FIX THIS: WHAT YOU NEED TO KNOW ABOUT GRIEF TO BE AN ALLY

I promise to respect your unique experience of grief and to focus on where I can help you find comfort and ease.

Before Will died, I was a true grief novice who made a lot of poor choices and assumptions when people around me experienced the death of their loved ones. I stayed silent when I should have said something. I used naive and ignorant phrases in an attempt to provide my loved ones with comfort. I thought that if people just embraced grief and felt everything that came with it then one day it would be over. I thought I understood what grief was, but I really didn't. I don't want you to make those same mistakes.

With science, technology, and western medicine, human beings have done incredible work in engineering ways to remove discomfort from the way we live. Our lives are full of tools and toys that distract us from feeling our feelings. There's medication for nearly every ailment we might experience, and when there isn't a cure, there are countless numbing agents accessible to us like food, alcohol, exercise, drugs, work, etc. Some of us are so good at denying and dismissing what is uncomfortable that we don't even realize that we're doing it. We soar right through the acknowledgment of what hurts on to our trusted methods for pain management. The usual sources of consolation are not going to work for grief, which stumps people who haven't had to experience it yet.

In fact, the first step in becoming a grief ally is simple to say but takes a minute to really understand: It is knowing that you cannot fix this. You cannot cure grief as if it were an illness or a broken bone that can be healed. Sure, you can send the flowers and a card. You can offer hugs and comedic relief, but these are tools to soothe the reactions and responses to grief. They work in the short term, but they're not a realistic approach for the long haul. As you move forward and watch your person take in what their life looks like now that their beloved is dead, you're going to find that flowers and humor fall short. You just can't fix their reality for them.

Understanding why you can't fix grief is the foundation of grief allyship. When you understand that grief isn't a problem to be solved but a truth to be integrated into your person's life, you'll change the way that you show up to help. In this chapter I'm going to walk you through the basics of what grief really is, why it's complex, and why everyone's experience of grief is unique. These ideas are the foundation that underpins grief allyship, and they illustrate why a long-term mindset is critical to supporting your person as they grieve the death of their beloved.

Grief Is All About Attachment

The first important thing to understand about grief is that its origin lies in attachment. We grieve as human beings because attachment is an involuntary part of our nature. What's more, it has been critical to the survival of our species. Our conditioning to attach starts before birth as babies attach to their mothers for the most essential roots of human development. John Bowlby (1907–1990), the father of attachment theory, determined that children come into the world biologically pre-programmed to form attachments with others.[3] Working closely with student Mary Ainsworth, Bowlby speculated and tested theories that children mourned separations from their primary caregivers. He ultimately took what he learned about attachment and separation and applied it to grief and bereavement in the final installment of his trilogy *Attachment and Loss*.[4]

How attachment loss is processed by our brains and bodies is what we call grief. In the revised edition of their book, *Grieving Beyond Gender: Understanding the Ways Men and Women Mourn*, Kenneth J. Doka and Terry L. Martin explain that grief is a reaction to loss and that grief itself is a physical energy created by "conflict between the world that was, what it cannot be, and how it may become that creates tensions that engender grief."[5]

That statement is important because it defines what grief actually is. Grief, at its core, is the involuntary internal physical energy of our brains and bodies contracting, expanding, shifting, changing, and trying to adjust to the severing of an attachment. What's also implicit to the statement is that the only thing that would cure your person's grief would be to have their beloved back, alive and well, but we both know that's not possible. That certainty is why grief can't be cured or fixed. On top of that, we as humans can be emotionally attached to more than just people. Places, projects, identities, and dreams are just a few examples. Because we can attach to tangible and intangible things, grief is neither simplistic nor one dimensional.

Grief Is Complex and Not Linear

You've probably heard of "The Five Stages of Grief."[6] This model is well-known and much used because it's easy to remember and plays into our desires to cure, fix, and clean up the messiness of grief. Unfortunately, despite being well-thought-out, the five stages (denial, anger, bargaining, depression, and acceptance) have been misunderstood for a very long time. They were never intended to be anticipatory or to be perceived as a checklist of experiences that, once checked off, signal that a griever is one step closer to their grief being over. On the contrary, those five steps are just a sampling of what someone *might* experience in their grief, and the chances of experiencing them in order and only once are slim. The risk in relying on the five stages of grief as a one-and-done matter is dismissing not only the profound experience of losing someone beloved but the multitude of losses that come after, as a consequence of that death, and the abundance of conflicting and simultaneous emotion that's generated because of all that loss.

When it comes to grieving, the primary loss—in your case, the death of your person's beloved—will inevitably escalate into a domino effect of *multiple* secondary losses. I like to use the metaphor of an earthquake to explain how these losses work.

The first shock is your person's beloved dying. The aftershocks are the secondary losses. They could be the unanticipated loss of future plans, changes in other relationships and communities because their beloved isn't an active member anymore, loss of routines and rituals, changes to fundamental beliefs about life, or even mundane day-to-day responsibilities, and much, much more. Like aftershocks, secondary losses happen over time in the days, months, and years after the primary loss, often getting stacked one on top of another.

In other words, your person isn't just experiencing grief because their beloved died. They're experiencing a multitude of losses because their beloved died. What's worse is that the aftershocks can take your person by surprise when they're already worn down or exhausted from trying to survive the initial quake, but secondary losses don't get the same attention as the primary loss. There aren't cultural ceremonies or often even formal acknowledgments when those related attachments change. But they still occur, and your person will feel each additional loss fully. Your person will remain painfully aware of these additional losses every time they find that circumstances have changed or ended or would have been different if their beloved was still alive. Moreover, they must deal with the secondary losses on top of having to try to survive in an environment that is still unstable and to which they haven't adjusted yet. These secondary losses accumulate on top of one another, compounding and changing your person's landscape over time. That's why grief is complex, and it's a huge part of why your person will need your support through the long haul.

Understanding how complex grief is, because of its layered losses over time, also demonstrates why grief isn't linear or simply a phase that's over after following a series of predetermined steps. Your person now lives with an energy inside them created by tensions between the world that existed when their beloved was alive, what life cannot be like anymore because their beloved is gone, and the ambiguity of the future in realizing that more loss is imminent. This tension gets recreated again and again as more secondary losses are recognized, layered on top of one another, and layered again onto a new life without their beloved—a reality in which your person likely wouldn't have ever chosen to live. Unfortunately, there isn't any framework, model, or series of stages that would give you certainty in how your person will react and respond to the energetic tension of their grief. No one can make assumptions like that because how your person will experience and express their grief depends on a multitude of factors.

Grief Looks and Feels Different for Everyone

The most common portrayal of grief is someone overwhelmed with sadness, but that image is a narrow expression of what it can actually look like. Don't assume that if your person isn't crying all the time or if they've returned to work that they aren't grieving anymore or they aren't grieving "appropriately." You know now that grief is complex and dynamic. So, too, are the ways your person will actually experience and express how they feel about their losses. One's surface disposition is dependent on a wide variety of psychological, social, cultural, and biological variables, all of which have the capacity to interact with one another.

In *Grieving Beyond Gender,* Doka and Martin propose that there are two distinct styles of how individuals express their grief: intuitive grief and instrumental grief.[7] The two styles of grief expression differ in how a person takes the internal energy created by grief and manifests it externally. The intuitive griever converts more of their energy into emotion. For the intuitive griever, their means of grief expression consists primarily of profoundly painful feelings; they feel before they think. They tend to spontaneously express their feelings and want to share those feelings with others. The intuitive griever does well in support-group settings. The instrumental griever, on the other hand, converts most of their energy into cognitive processing. For them, grief is more of an intellectual experience. They may also prefer to discuss problems rather than their feelings.

Those two different styles of grieving exist on a continuum, and the majority of people experience and express their grief in ways common to both styles but towards either end of the continuum. Whether grievers are intuitive or instrumental or blended depends on whether they feel first, meaning they're a more intuitive griever, or think first, meaning they're a more instrumental griever, or they experience a fairly equal portion of both. You can hypothesize your person's place in the continuum by their willingness to talk about their feelings rather than their issues, and whether they are more focused on difficulties related to how they feel or on solving external problems created by their loss.[8] Ultimately, though, your person will grieve in the way that makes the most sense to them if you give them the space and respect to do so.

I want you to know that grief expression is unique to everyone so that you can avoid any harmful assumptions. If your person isn't overwhelmed with emotion or isn't willing to share their feelings, that doesn't mean that they aren't grieving or grieving "appropriately." Respecting your person and their losses means respecting how they'll express their grief too. There's a risk of generating unnecessary distress for your person if they're not given the space needed to grieve in the way that feels right to them. They don't need any extra burden. Grief is already stressful at a basic level.

Assume This Will Last Forever

Now that you know that grief can't be fixed and that the death of your person's beloved isn't the only loss that they'll experience, you know that the tensions that engender grief can last forever. Your person now has a reference for what was, what is, and what can and cannot happen in the future. That outlook isn't a sensation that can be forgotten or that anyone can get over or move on from. Your person will not wake up after the funeral healed and ready to jump back into their life like nothing ever happened. The triangle-shape sandwiches might be tasty, but they are not magical.

Consider, for example, what it would look and feel like if your home, neighborhood, city, or your whole world collapsed in an earthquake. You'd likely be stunned as you see it in a completely different state. What once was can now be barely recognizable. It might take a very long time before you're even comfortable with walking up to touch it. And then when you begin exploring, you're climbing around on what is remaining. The terrain, although familiar, is foreign and unstable. You have to be cautious about nearly every step, and even when you are, you might slip, get yourself caught up in the wreckage, or fall despite being alert. The chances are high that you might even need support in getting yourself unstuck from whatever situation you've fallen into.

There's a reason that specialists are called in after an earthquake: The landscape that remains in the midst of—and after—a natural disaster is risky, hazardous, and unpredictable. Living with the loss of someone they love comes with all of the same unpredictability for your person. That said, cities, with thoughtful care and attention, do get rebuilt over time. Some things can't be restored, but some buildings and bridges can be. A city after an earthquake is still a city, but it's a changed one. The same will be true for your person when you can offer them similar thoughtful care and attention.

Instead of moving on, getting over, or healing grief, your person will move forward with it, carrying it, growing around it, and relating to it as they age and through everything they experience after the moment their beloved died. Hope Edelman says it best on the cover of her book, *The AfterGrief*: "Whether we want it to or not, grief gets folded into our developing identities, where it informs our thoughts, hopes, expectations, behaviors, and fears, as we inevitably carry it forward into everything that follows."[9]

With time—think years, not days or weeks—your person will rebuild their life around the legacy of their beloved. They'll find a way to live around it and coexist with the pain that comes with missing someone who should be here as well as the life they cannot have now because they're gone. But to be able to do that, they need you. Helping them live around their losses is where you have power. It is where the true work of grief allyship begins.

What Is Grief Allyship?

You can help create the conditions that your person needs to make sense of the many, many losses that they'll experience because they've lost their beloved. You can be the person in their life who understands why they won't move on or get over their grief. You can respect that your person's grief is unlike anyone else's experience of grief. You can allow them to express their grief in the ways that feel right for them, without judgment or criticism. You can be a safe space that respects the time it will take for your person to integrate all the changes in their life that will occur because of their many losses.

> *Grief Allyship is the act of supporting and advocating for those who are grieving by providing unconditional love, empowerment, and deep reverence.*

Being a grief ally means loving your person through every reaction and response they'll experience in their grief; validating all the emotions they'll feel upon their primary loss and as secondary losses unfold; being willing to bear witness to everything without trying to fix any of it; and respecting your person's deeply personal process of coping with and integrating the loss into their life.

Helping Begins Here

At this point, you're probably asking yourself, "What do I do?" and "How do I help?" The answer to those questions lies in the last lesson I have to share about the nature of grief, which is that it is *exhausting*.

Grief will exhaust your person. For a long time, their grief could consume them. Their brain will be tied up with building new neural pathways trying to make sense of a new reality without their beloved in it. And while they do that, they'll be bumped up against by naive grief support from others, maybe a lot of paperwork, and memory after memory of how life used to be. On top of all of it, they are still a human being with human needs and commitments: food, hydration, basic hygiene, water, shelter, sleep, parenting, pet parenting, care and upkeep of their home, income generation, etc. Having to do all of that on top of experiencing tensions of their competing losses adds to their life stressors.

So, taking what you've learned in this chapter, knowing that you cannot fix their grief, what can you do? You can make their life easier and more comfortable. As your person takes in their losses and, over time, learns how to integrate them into their new reality, ask yourself these questions:

> *How, in this moment, on this day, can I make my person's life any easier?*
>
> *How can I make them more comfortable?*

You do not have to be a grief expert to be a grief ally. You can just focus on bringing comfort and ease to your person. But you do need to be capable of existing in an environment that is unpredictable and changes frequently. I'll teach you how to do that in the next chapter.

Comfort and Ease: Ideas for How to Be a Grief Ally

- **Identify your strengths and assets.**

    Make a master list of your strengths and assets that you can return to over and over. Consider what you have or what you're already good at that would help make your person's life easier and more comfortable during this time and going forward. Where can you apply your existing skills and resources? You don't have to cook if you're not that great in the kitchen. Maybe you're an amazing notetaker? An epic proofreader or writer who can help with a eulogy, important announcements, or meaningful responses to messages? Great with pets? Or with kids? Do you have access to a hot tub? Keep an open mind as you brainstorm.

- **Improve your grief literacy.**

    At the end of this book, I've included a list of the resources that I trust to speak honestly and intentionally about grief. If you want more information about grief, I would start there.

- **Share this book with others.**

    Let others know what you've learned. Encourage those who want to help your person to read this book. Remember that the quality of your person's social support network is a powerful indicator of how well they'll be able to cope with and to grow and recover from the death of their beloved. If everyone who is supporting your person knows that, your person's future will be so much easier and more comfortable.

CHAPTER 3

YOU CAN'T TAKE CARE OF YOUR PERSON IF YOU AREN'T CARING FOR YOURSELF

I promise to take good care of myself so that I can take good care of you.

In the days after Will died, I noticed a theme among the people who showed up to help me. In the rush to get to my side, a number of them showed up panicked and distraught with an uneasiness painted across their face that read, "I am deeply uncomfortable, but instead of tending to what I'm feeling, I'm just going to show up and do everything that I can for you—hold you, cook for you, shop for you, drink for you, sit on your couch for you, feed you, fly to you, call you, talk to you…" despite the fact that I asked for very little of that. To be frank, at that time my body hadn't yet begun to feel the severity of what would happen to my life, and being surrounded by so many people was overwhelming. When it comes to your role as a grief ally, I want you to do something different.

As you witness your person's grief, I want you to be equally invested in your own well-being as much as you are invested in theirs. Taking care of your own body and mind might seem selfish at this moment, but I promise you that it is not. Making your own well-being a priority will ensure that you stay healthy while you're present to one of the most disruptive experiences any human being can endure. By taking care of your own emotional needs as they arise, you'll be able to remain present to your person and their experience. And you'll be able to do that for as long as they need you. Ignoring your own feelings and needs isn't okay and comes with significant consequences that can make you physically and mentally ill. If you aren't healthy, you are not going to be able to help your person. I've broken down what I want you to do into three steps that I'll teach you in this chapter: self-awareness, self-expression, and self-compassion. When you can follow these steps, you'll be supporting your person from a place of strength and stability.

Be a Super Human, Not a Superhero

The aftermath of a tragedy is a really stressful situation, and all human bodies have a unique way of responding to stress. Biology is important here. For starters, our bodies become flooded with stress hormones, like adrenaline, that help us respond to the imminent threat. In order to survive, our ability to feel pain is reduced, our digestive systems shut down, and our brains become hypervigilant, concentrating exclusively on what can harm us. In this state, we're expending incredible energy, but our brains cannot rest because they're consumed with evading whatever is putting us at risk. That biological reaction is vital when it comes to helping us escape burning buildings, fighting back when we're being attacked, or performing first aid after a car accident. The experience of this kind of state is short. When you're out of danger, your body can return to its normal, regulated state where you can eat, sleep, and think like you did before.

One thing to be aware of from the start is that this superhero biological response is impossible to maintain in the context of grief support, even though grief can be a crisis that keeps on giving.

The body's stress response system is meant to help us survive *short-term* life-threatening situations. Helpful and respectful grief support for your person is not a short-term commitment or an imminent threat that can be escaped, but your body might not be able to make that distinction right away. Your amygdala, the oldest and most animalistic part of your brain where your stress responses originate, may have helped you drop in like a superhero when you first received the news that that your person's beloved died—to hold, clean, cook, shop, sit, drink, feed, etc. But what you did in superhero mode, while your body was flooded with stress hormones and screaming at you to DO SOMETHING, was to create an outlet for your body's stress response.

As a grief ally, you first need to be able to recognize when your nervous system is going into superhero mode. You also have to learn to discern when superhero mode is going to be helpful and when it isn't. At times it might be useful. If your person signals for help because of being cornered by a naive relative at the funeral home babbling about just moving on to a new beloved, by all means, jump in and be a superhero. But at many other moments, you will have to learn to be someone whose superpower is just *being present* and *supportive* as your person grapples with the really shitty reality that death is permanent and that grief can change everything. Trying to be the other kind of superhero can't save you—or your person—from those feelings.

Superheroes are fueled by extraterrestrial potions, crystals, and imagination; they don't need the kind of fuel that we do to survive. Like all human beings, you need food, water, shelter, and rest, among other things, to stay alive. You also need to avoid chronic stress to stay healthy. Being in a situation where your body is constantly flooded with stress hormones has unhealthy consequences. Chronic stress can cause or contribute to a number of physical and mental illnesses such as depression, anxiety, heart disease, sleep issues, addiction, ulcers, colitis, and more.[10] You are not going to be able to be there for your person through the long haul if you're suffering from the consequences of trying to be a superhero for too long. That's why grief allyship requires a specific kind of self-care.

When you start feeling like you need to be a superhero, I want you to pause and focus on yourself for a moment. Self-care as a grief ally requires tuning in to what you are feeling and experiencing because of this death in your community. It requires that you grieve what was and what will change because your person's beloved died. It requires that you listen to your body and do your best to give it what it needs to show up for your person. It means being a *super human* not a superhero. That work begins with being aware of what you're feeling as a grief ally.

Self-Awareness: What Are You Feeling?

To show up for your person through the long haul of their loss, you are going to have to be present for the entirety of their grief. It's possible that you will witness some of life's deepest, darkest, and most chaotic emotions on top of observing the hardest truth of being human: that one day everyone dies. There won't be anything you can do to change it. Putting yourself in a position that confronts the truth of our mortality is vulnerable and uncomfortable, but there isn't a way to be a grief ally without going there. Grief allyship is courageous work because you are voluntarily putting yourself in an environment rife with potentially distressing emotions. On top of that, grief will change your person, which means that it will create changes in your relationship with them as well.

That reality sucks. It's not fair to you that your relationship with your person is going to be different. It's not fair that your person's beloved is dead. I know that, and it's okay to feel robbed, angry, hurt, frustrated, sad, or a kaleidoscope of other things about all this change that's happening and is going to happen in your life. But to be able to tolerate it or accept it without doing significant harm to yourself requires that you give these feelings some attention.

Self-awareness is the foundation for how to take care of yourself as a grief ally. To be self-aware means becoming alert and knowledgeable about what it is that you're actually feeling. Feelings are signals that our bodies send our brain about what we need moment to moment to care for ourselves. These might be physical things like water or food, or emotional things like love, affection, or affirmation. If you're not aware of what you're feeling, you won't know what you need in order to be capable of being present with your person. You'll become rundown, unregulated, unhealthy, and ultimately unhelpful.

In practice, self-awareness is simply getting into the habit of naming the emotion that you're experiencing. Sweaty palms, an increasing heart rate, heat rising in your cheeks, tension in your jaw, or lumps in your throat all are examples of biological signals. The brain receives signals from the body constantly. When you start to listen to those signals, you can begin to define them and name them as feelings.

Here's an exercise you can do to help you practice being more self-aware of what you're feeling at any given time.

You will need:

- A piece of paper and pen, the note app on your phone, or a quiet place where you can talk out loud to yourself.
- A feeling wheel (*optional*). (They're all over the internet. Find one that you like. My favorite is from The Junto Institute.)

Instructions:

- As time passes and you spend time supporting your person, reflect on what you're feeling. Listen, watch, and feel for signals from your body.
- When your body is feeling uncomfortable, weird, or you feel yourself transforming into the Hulk, take a moment for yourself in a quiet place or pull out something to write on.
- Try to find a name for what it is you're feeling or felt in that moment. Can you name that feeling?
- If you can't find the word instantly, look at a feeling wheel. With its help, can you name that feeling now?
- Write down what you're feeling or say it out loud, which might look/sound like:

I feel inadequate.
I feel overwhelmed.
I feel relieved.

I feel enraged.
I feel ignored.

Being aware of what it is that you're feeling sets the foundation for self-care. Your feelings, if you're listening to them, will point you toward what it is that you really need in order to take care of yourself as you bear witness to your person's grief.

Self-Expression: What to Do with Your Feelings

After you've honed the skill of being more aware of what you're feeling, you can move onto the next step in the self-care process: self-expression. Now, I don't mean running to tell anyone who will listen about your feelings, although that might be what you need sometimes. What I want you to be able to do is to listen to your body and discover what you need to do to express your feelings. Then, I want you to do that thing, or a variation of it. That's what I mean by self-expression, and by practicing self-expression you're actively working to regulate your nervous system, giving yourself more capacity to be present to your person and their pain.

Self-expression is critical because not acknowledging your own emotions can be really harmful. Avoiding your feelings, bottling them up, or swallowing them can be really detrimental to your mental and physical health. In the book *It's Not Always Depression,* noted author and therapist Hilary Jacobs Handel writes,

> "Most of us don't know how to deal with emotions effectively. Instead, we work hard to manage them through avoidance. That coping strategy is the very thing that leads to symptoms of

mental distress such as depression and anxiety. Avoiding emotions just does not work in the long run."[11]

Feelings can be distressing, but they are just feelings. You are not hurting anyone or anything by having them, but you *will* hurt yourself in the long run if you let them fester inside of you. And if you are hurting, how will you be helpful to your person?

As an extension of the self-awareness exercise in the above section, we're going to add on a self-expression piece. If you reflect back on what you've learned about self- awareness and remember that your body is constantly sending you signals that we define as feelings, I want you to train yourself to interpret your feelings as defining a need. You'll be surprised by your own inner wisdom when you simply ask yourself the right questions. When you can interpret what your body is telling you that it needs, you can become the expert in having those needs met too. Your feelings know what they need you to do to express them. You just need to practice listening.

Practicing Self-Expression

Returning to our self-awareness exercise, let's add the next steps for recognizing what we need to do to express what we're feeling.

After you name a feeling, try completing this sentence:

- I am feeling ____ so I need ____.

Some examples might include:

- *I am feeling <u>enraged</u> so I need <u>to scream.</u>*
- *I am feeling <u>lonely</u> so I need <u>to talk about what I'm feeling.</u>*

- *I am feeling <u>worn out</u> so I need <u>rest.</u>*
- *I am feeling <u>overwhelmed</u> so I need <u>slow and thoughtful breathing.</u>*
- *I am feeling <u>nervous</u> so I need <u>to move my body.</u>*

Once you're able to answer the "*so I need _____*" part of this exercise, the next step is to simply do what you can to fulfill that need.

In case you find yourself stumped for what it is that you need based on what you're feeling, I've created a list of ideas to get you started. Maybe you'll find something here that works great, or maybe reviewing this list will just get you thinking in the right direction. When you're feeling a big emotion, but you don't know what it is that you really need, return to this list and let it inspire you.

Ideas for What You Might Need to Do with Your Feelings

- Talk to someone you trust
- Write in a journal
- Color
- Let out a scream or primal roar
- Read books
- Stomp your feet
- Paint
- Meditate
- Do a body scan

- Practice yoga
- Go for a walk
- Practice breath-relaxation work
- Chop wood
- Do some research
- Cut the grass
- Sing at the top of your lungs
- Have a cup of tea
- Write letters you might never send
- Dance it out
- Take a nap
- Speak to a therapist or a coach
- Have a good cry
- Take a shower
- Have a snack
- Go to bed early
- Walk away
- Say "no" to someone

Your action to take care of yourself can be big or small. It might also require some creativity. What you can do to meet your needs will also depend on where you are, your resources, and your abilities. If you're in the same room as others, it might not be feasible to start screaming at the very moment you determine that a scream is necessary. You might want to excuse yourself to howl into a pillow or at the very least invite the other people in your presence to join you in a roar. What's important is that you know what you need and that you can express that need. Sometimes that acknowledgement is enough to let your body relax a little so that you can be present for your person again. Other times you will have to go all the way and get what your body is telling you is necessary.

I understand that if you are present with your person when big feelings crop up, you might not be able to do what you need for yourself at that moment. If you can't, make a note of it and do your best to give your feelings the attention they need later. That ability is an important skill to develop for a variety of situations we find ourselves in when we deal with challenges or adversity. In the meantime, you might find it tempting to confide in your person about what you're experiencing, but please don't do that. I know that they are your person and before their beloved died you would have told them anything, but it's important to recognize that right now they won't be able to help you. To determine whom you can go to if you need to talk to someone, I suggest using Ring Theory.

Ring Theory and How Not to Say the Wrong Thing

Ring Theory was created by Susan Silk, a clinical psychologist, and Barry Goldman, an arbitrator, mediator, and author. It's a simple tool that was popularized in a 2013 *LA Times* article,[12] and you can use it to figure out the right person to go to with your feelings. Here's how to use it.

Draw a small circle on a piece of paper. This is the center ring. In it, put the name of your person, since they're the person

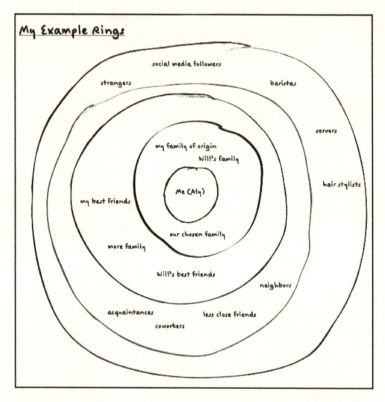

at the center of the current crisis. Now, draw a larger circle around the first one. In that ring put the name of the person or people next closest to the crisis. That might be your person's children, siblings, parents, or members of their chosen family. You might also belong in the second ring. Repeat the process as many times as you need to. In each larger ring put the next closest people. Immediate family members typically come before more distant relatives, and intimate friends go in the smaller rings whereas less intimate friends go in the larger ones. Remember, though, that not all families are alike. Blood relations aren't guaranteed to be in a smaller circle. Your person's circles will be unique to them. You can see the rings of my community that I've included here as an example. At the end of this drawing process, you'll have a Kvetching Order, or a complaining order. Based on this Kvetching Order, Silk and Goldman state that the following are the rules:

> "The person in the center ring can say anything she wants to anyone, anywhere. She can kvetch and complain and whine and moan and curse the heavens and say, "Life is unfair" and "Why me?" That's the one payoff for being in the center ring. Everyone else can say those things too, but only to people in larger rings. [...] If you want to scream or cry or complain, if you want to tell someone how shocked you are or how icky you feel, or whine about how it reminds you of all the terrible things that have happened to you lately, that's fine. It's a perfectly normal response. Just do it to someone in a bigger ring"[13]

Your feelings are valid and worthy of attention as you practice being a grief ally, but if you need to share them with someone, make sure you're sharing with the right person. The great thing about using Ring Theory is that you're starting out having already limited your opportunities to say the wrong thing to the wrong person while also taking care of your own needs. The rule to remember here is to always vent and complain to people further from the center of the tragedy than where you are.

What to Do When You Can't Get What You Need

The last note that I have about self-expression is that you might not be able to get or do what it is that your body is telling you that you need. In situations like those, I suggest two questions: First, is there a next-best thing? For example, if your body is telling you that you are angry and you need to break something but that's either not possible or is inadvisable, can you try stomping your feet instead? Or punching couch cushions? If there isn't a next-best thing and what you actually need is something you cannot do or someone you don't have access to, ask yourself this second question: Is what you're feeling is actually grief?

You know now that grief is a physical energy created by tensions between what was and what is and wanting it to be different. It's very likely that if your person is changing because of the death of their beloved, the relationship that they have with you will change too. Experiencing your own grief as a grief ally is normal and okay. What's important is that you remember that grief cannot be fixed. Instead, focus on what I've taught you. What can you do to bring yourself comfort and ease? One suggestion that I, myself, have to do is the last step in this self-care process: Offer yourself some compassion.

Self-Compassion: Everything You're Feeling Is Okay

As you bear witness to your person's grief, it's going to be tempting to minimize your own feelings. It's also going to be easy to compare your losses to your person's and believe that their reality is worse than yours. While that might be true, I want to urge you to give yourself permission to acknowledge whatever feelings *you have* as a result of this death as well. That's what self-compassion is in the context of grief allyship: allowance and acceptance that you will have your own thoughts, feelings, and experiences in this role and give yourself permission to recognize them.

We cannot change the fact that death makes everyone feel

defenseless. It reminds us that we are mortal and that one day we all will die. Death warns us that the time we have with the people we love is finite. Death can shake us from the belief that we have control over everything in our lives. And if we haven't given ourselves time to grieve other losses in our lives, a death within your social circle might bring up old wounds that need your attention. On top of these truths, grief support is vulnerable and uncomfortable work that requires incredible physical, mental, and emotional endurance.

As a grief ally, you will be present to big and painful emotions, and you'll have to be able to exist in an environment that you cannot control. In that environment you're bound to make some mistakes simply because you've never done it before and because you're learning as you go. These conditions can destabilize even the most level-headed of individuals, and that's why you have to be really kind to yourself while you're in this role.

I know you can be compassionate because if you weren't you wouldn't be on the hunt to be the best kind of support for your person as they grieve. The trick is to be able to extend that love and generosity to *yourself* as well. You would not turn your person away at this difficult moment in their life, so don't turn away from your own feelings and needs either. Acknowledging your own feelings is how you can practice self-compassion.

You do not have to be stoic to be a grief ally. In fact, I'd warn against trying to endure your experience in this front-row seat to bereavement without any complaining or acknowledgement of your own feelings. You know now that ignoring or suppressing your feelings can be detrimental to your physical and mental health. If you do not let yourself feel and express anything about what you're witnessing and experiencing you're going to limit your ability to help your person. By allowing yourself to have feelings and being mindful about having your needs met, you're going to be able to show up for your person for the long haul. On airplanes they tell you to put your own oxygen mask on first; in grief allyship, you have to take care of yourself so that you can take good care of the people that you love.

Practicing Self-Compassion

Here's a new exercise you can do to remind yourself to be as kind and caring to yourself as you are to your person. Completing this exercise will hopefully remind you, as you witness that your person and their life is changing, that you are allowed to be moved by it all, and that taking good care of yourself will help you remain in your grief ally role.

You'll need something to write on and something to write with, whether that's paper and a pen, your laptop, or the note app on your phone.

- Write yourself a note giving yourself permission to have feelings about what you're experiencing. In the note, tell yourself that your feelings are just tools to tell you what you need so that you can continue to show up for your person.

I get that this exercise might sound basic or even silly, but it's an important gesture of self-kindness. By letting yourself be moved by what you're experiencing and making sure that your own needs are met, you can be more present for your person and their needs as well.

Over time, as you continue to help your person through the long haul of their grief, you can return to this exercise when you find yourself feeling really big emotions. A little reminder to yourself that you're allowed to have feelings and time to deal with them goes a long way.

A Healthy Grief Ally Is the Best Grief Ally

Grief allyship is not an easy role, but it is one of the most important ones that you will ever embody in your lifetime. In order to show up for your person through the long haul of their loss, you are allowing yourself to be uncomfortable and to feel vulnerable, which is why this is courageous work. You're going to have to coexist with distressing thoughts and feelings. You're going to have to accept that you will make mistakes. But by practicing self-awareness, self-expression, and having compassion for yourself, you're going to be able to remain present throughout the entirety of your person's grief while also taking good care of yourself.

It's also okay to be afraid. If you've never been in this role before, all the unknowns can be scary, but let me tell you something: Even if you do have grief support on your resume, every time that you show up to help someone through the long haul of their grief, you'll have to do it differently. You know why now, right? Because grief looks and feels different for everyone. So, even if you've been in this role before, don't let false security make you think what has been helpful for one person might also be helpful for another. You have to let your person be the expert in their own grief.

Comfort and Ease: Ideas for How to Be a Grief Ally

- **Sketch your own Ring Theory diagram.**

    Based on Ring Theory, make a list of all the people who are in the outer rings. Keep this list on hand so that if or when you need to talk to someone about what you're experiencing, you know who are the right people to go to. Don't be afraid to seek out your own support to cope with this death in your community.

- **Write your person's beloved a letter.**

    In the letter, tell them how you're feeling, what you think your person is feeling, or what you're witnessing in your grief support role. This exercise is a lot like journaling, except that you're directing your thoughts and feelings to someone specific. You don't have to share this letter with anyone. It might just feel good as something for you to do for yourself at this moment.

- **Learn more about self-care.**

    If the concept of making your well-being a priority is new to you, do more research. Seek out resources that will teach you more about what it means to take good care of yourself.

CHAPTER 4

ALLIES, NOT ENEMIES: HOW TO BE PART OF YOUR PERSON'S SUPPORT TEAM

I promise to trust you as the expert of your own grief, to respect your team, and to love you unconditionally always.

The Parking Lot Blowout

"So, I kind of had an argument with your mom," said April, my college roommate and friend of 12 years, as she walked me out of the funeral home into a dark parking lot. It was Day Three. Three days since Will had died. Two days since my mom and April had arrived at my one-bedroom apartment. One day since my siblings had flown across the country to be there too. And today, we'd all been ushered into a room at the funeral home and sat perched on the edges of sterile furniture while decisions were made.

The funeral director had spoken matter-of-factly, taking notes as I answered his questions. Venue? Check. Flowers? Whites and greens. Food? We'll need gluten-free options. Open casket or closed? You'll have to deliver clothes for his body by Tuesday morning. Here are the variety of urns we have available. Which one would you like? He spoke as though offering different ice cream flavors rather than a capsule for what would remain of my beloved's body when all that was left was ashes. I rested on the edge of an armchair with my shoulders hunched and my eyes on the ground, sometimes open but mostly closed. None of us had ever had to do this before, cope with the aftermath of a tragedy like this one. And after three days in superhero mode, composure was waning amongst the people who love me the most.

April didn't have to tell me what happened. Having felt the conflict building over the last three days, I knew *exactly* why a fight had erupted: rivalry and tensions over who thought they had the right to be helping me, who wanted to be the leader, and who thought they knew me the best. Sensing this storm brewing, I'd tried to keep all the helping hands busy, tried to keep things peaceful. Some listened, but others heard what they wanted to hear. By Day Three, my efforts proved futile. In my absence, words were slung at one another by my loved ones. Feelings were hurt and cars peeled out of the funeral home parking lot. April booked a flight home the next day, and I hid in my closet for the rest of the night.

Underneath our coats and camping equipment, I called a 24-hour crisis line. I didn't have the energy to be a referee. I just wanted all the fighting to stop. I wanted to rewind to Tuesday and tell Will not to leave. All I wanted was Will, alive.

Grief Allyship Isn't a One-Person Job

Conflicts are apt to happen in moments of emotional distress, and that's okay. Shock, anxiety, stress, and grief, combined with changes to your environment, sleep, routine, and having to spend time in uncomfortable situations are perfect conditions for disagreements to become full-blown screaming matches. Unfortunately, though, conflict between the people who want to help isn't what your person needs in the immediate aftermath of a major loss.

Grief allyship isn't a one-person job. It will take a team to help your person survive the loss of their beloved. You are certainly a member of that team, and an important one, but it's more important to recognize that you are not the only one. When you practice grief allyship with a focus on working as a team with the other close people in their life, your person will feel loved and supported. If you don't, the consequence is typically friction piling more stress and upset on your person during an already incredibly difficult time.

This chapter is going to teach you how to be an effective member of your person's grief support team. I'll cover the strategies and mindset that you, your person, and the others who want to help can adopt to create the best conditions for your person to get exactly what they need to cope with their grief. It's my hope that if you put these lessons into practice, you'll avoid having your own parking lot blowout and that your person will only have to sleep in their closet if they *want* to.

Your Person Is the Expert, So Be a Front-Row Student

Reflecting back on what you've learned about grief so far, you know that your person's experience of it is entirely unique to them. Only they know what their grief looks and feels like. If the death of their beloved was unexpected, it will take time for them to become acquainted with *this thing* they'll carry with them forever. Only your person can be the expert in their unique experience of grief, and because of that, you need to empower them to embody that role. When you believe that your person is the expert, your approach to helping should be to learn everything you can about what they're feeling and going through without assumptions or preconceived notions. Let their unique experience of grief be your classroom, and within it be a front-row student.

Being a front-row student isn't complicated in theory, but it takes heaps of vulnerability, courage, humility, and patience to be able to stay there. Alan Wolfelt PhD, a death educator and grief counselor who leads the Center for Loss & Life Transition in Fort Collins, Colorado, teaches this technique and calls it companioning.[14] Wolfelt advocates that the role of a grief caregiver is not about assessing, analyzing, fixing, or resolving your person's grief but rather maintaining a willingness to learn and stay present. A front-row student takes in everything that the subject expert (your person, in this case) has to offer and asks questions when they don't understand. They're eager to learn from their mistakes because they want the knowledge that the expert has to offer. They know the value in what they're learning and are willing to dive deeper into the subject. That's what it means to be in the front row in all things in life, including as a grief ally.

You now know that this loss could change your person, but what you don't know is how they'll act under this kind of stress or what they'll need moment to moment to cope with it. You don't know how different they'll be as they learn to live around the void with which their beloved has left them. You can't assume what your person wants and needs without intentionally being present with them in their grief. You can't assume that your person's experience is going to be the same as anyone else's. The best assumption that you can make is that you don't know them at all anymore. Starting there demands that you learn how your person is uniquely experiencing the death of their beloved. Staying there will help ensure your success at being a grief ally. At the same time, you also have to remember that you are not the only one in your person's classroom.

Teamwork Can Be Tough

Chances are, you are not the only one who wants to help your person during this time. For your person, that's a really great thing. More love is more love. And love feels so damn good for a broken heart. Given that grief lasts forever, your person will need a team to help them cope with the death of their beloved and all the loss that might come afterward. Grief allyship is too heavy, too intense, and too long to be done alone. In order for you to be able to be a grief ally through the long haul, you are going to have to work with a team. Sometimes when many people all love and want to help the same person it can feel like you're all competing with one another. But here, when your person is grieving the death of their beloved, there's no room for competition.

Putting yourself in competition with others who want to support your person makes grief support about you. Here's the thing, though. It isn't about you. Grief allyship is about helping your person survive. There are only a few ways to fail at grief allyship, and believing that you are the best one or the only one or the right one to help your person? Yeah, that's one of them.

The reality is that *no one* is entitled to be a member of someone's support team. You might be tempted to believe that you have the right to be there if you're biologically related or you've held the coveted title of best friend at some point in your person's life. Sadly, blood or history might not guarantee that you will be called on to help your person or determine when that will be. Just know that if you want a spot on the team at all, how you handle being on the bench matters.

Lead from the Bench

Supporting your person doesn't always mean being the one who is with them in the moment. Sometimes support looks like respecting your person's decision to lean on other people in their network. When that is the case, I want you to think about what teamwork looks like from that position. Teamwork is a constant practice as well as a mindset. And when it comes to illustrating great teamwork there's nothing like a good sports analogy. So, let me tell you a story about Abby Wambach, the greatest soccer player of all time.

Abby Wambach won two gold medals at the Olympics and a FIFA World Cup title. She was the U.S. leading scorer in the 2007 and 2011 Women's World Cup tournaments, as well as in the 2004 and 2012 Olympics. She also held the rank of number one as highest all-time international goal scorer until January 2020. Abby Wambach is practically superhuman on the soccer field. But she's also an icon for the kind of teamwork that we should all aspire to practice.

In her 2019 book, *WOLFPACK: How to Come Together, Unleash Our Power, and Change the Game*, Wambach reflects on her experience of preparing for the 2015 FIFA Women's World Cup tournament. At that time, Wambach was co-captain of the U.S. Women's National team, and in that role, she was responsible for helping to decide how the team was going to win. She planned to make sure the team left the World Cup that year as champions, but early in the process of deciding which 11 players would give Team USA the best chance of winning, it became clear that Wambach wasn't one of them. In *WOLFPACK*, she writes:

> "So, imagine this: You've scored more international goals than any human being on the planet. You've co-captained and led Team USA to victory after victory for the last decade. And you and your coach sit down and decide together that you won't be a starter for the remainder of your final World Cup. Instead, you'll come from off the bench."[15]

Wambach admits the reality of the situation was hard to accept but recognized that if she didn't start on the bench, she would have missed out on the most important lesson of leadership: leading from the bench. Leading from the bench meant making her performance at the 2015 World Cup about the team and not about her. She still gave everything she had to the game but from a different position than ever before.

> "I paid attention. I screamed so loudly, obnoxiously, and relentlessly that the coach moved me to the far side of the bench. I kept water ready for the players coming off the field. I celebrated when goals were scored, and I kept believing in us even when mistakes were made. I knew the women on the field like sisters, so I could predict, in every moment, exactly what each needed from me. Whatever it was - comfort, encouragement, tough love, instruction - I offered it. At the end of that game, I was so exhausted, it was like I played all 90 minutes. The starters had left it all on the field; I left it all on the bench."[16]

That year, Team USA won the FIFA Women's World Cup. Abby Wambach and the 22 other players on Team USA—playing on the field and leading from the bench—won the World Cup, *together*.

Abby's lesson here is simple. Teamwork is more than what you do when you're on the field and playing in the game. Of course, being in the game and playing your best is the ultimate goal. It's what you prepare and train to do. But no matter where you are, you are always on the team. So, wherever you are, lead from there.

Your person needs you to approach your grief allyship just like Abby Wambach approached the World Cup. Not being the one in the moment with your person doesn't mean you should throw up your hands and walk away or believe that you are in competition with the person who has been called in to help. Instead, cheer for your team. Support your team. Believe in the team on which your person is relying to cope with their changing reality.

Empower Your Person to Be the Expert

"Tell me what's going on, Aly," my therapist said on the other end of the line as I paced back and forth in my driveway on the morning after The Parking Lot Blowout. With my phone pressed into my face, I watched the windows of my house, worried that what I was saying would be overheard by the audience inside.

"I hid in my closet last night," I replied. "Everyone is fighting, and I can't make it stop. I can't take it. I don't know what to do." I'd reached a tipping point. I couldn't handle the tension anymore. Until this point, I'd tried to be kind and respectful of everyone who wanted to help, but it wasn't working. It was making my situation worse.

Hearing the distress in my voice, my therapist asked, "Aly, is it okay to call what's happening to you traumatic? Is Will's death a traumatic event?"

"Um, sure. I guess so." Will's death was an accident while out on a hike. He was a healthy man doing something we'd done together countless times and never considered it to be life-threatening. His body wasn't able to be retrieved until 24 hours after he'd died. I laid awake in our bed after getting the news of his death, thinking about his body alone on the ground waiting to be recovered. I wondered what happened to the human body without a heartbeat in negative temperatures and high winds. I hadn't yet put the word *traumatic* to my experience, but it resonated in that moment.

"What we know about trauma recovery," my therapist's words broke through my troubled thoughts, "is that you're going to have the best chances of being *okay-ish* at some point if your post-event experiences are positive."

"Okay," I said.

It's worth nothing that therapists don't typically use pointed statements. At this moment, though, mine knew exactly what I needed to be told. They said: "Aly, you need to ask for exactly what you need. You need to do what is best for *you* right now."

"But what about hurting other people's feelings?" I asked. In hindsight, such worry is a sign of someone fawning in a crisis. I was ignoring my own needs and boundaries to satisfy the needs of others around me.

"I know you care a lot about other people, but right now you need to focus on yourself and your survival," they said. "Let other people deal with their own feelings for now. You're not responsible for them."

"Alright," I agreed hesitantly.

"Are there people in your life whom you can trust to respect every decision you make? Who will make mistakes and keep showing up because they'll always love you? Who will love you no matter what you ask of them? Even if it's to step back?"

"Yes."

"That's who you need right now. Call them, okay?"

That moment changed the course of my grief experience. Only your person knows what their grief feels like. Only your person can truly know what it is that they need to cope with all the feelings, sensations, losses, and change that will come along with it too. Because of that intimacy, your person needs to be respected as the only expert and encouraged to do whatever is best for them. Part of your responsibility as a grief ally is to respect whatever their choices are and to love your person unconditionally.

In *The Body Keeps the Score: Brain, Mind, and Body in the Healing of Trauma*, Bessel Van der Kolk MD. writes that being able to do something to protect oneself is a critical piece in determining whether or not a traumatic experience will leave long-lasting psychological scars.[17] Simply translated, it means that if your person is able to safely express their wants and needs right now and through the long haul of their grief, they'll have a greater likelihood of being *okay-ish* again one day. That outcome makes you and your teammates very important.

Just how important that outcome is became especially true for me. In the days after Will's death, what I really needed from the people who said they were there to support me was to know that they loved me no matter what. I needed them to empower me like my therapist empowered me. I needed them to ask questions when they didn't understand, and then I needed them to hear what I was saying. I needed them to trust and respect that I knew what I needed, from whom I needed it, and that everyone would still love me regardless of what I asked for and from whom. That's what your person needs from you too.

Your person's needs will continue to evolve as they move into a future without their beloved. So, settle into that front row. Stay engaged in the classroom. Keep your person empowered and loved unconditionally. And if you feel like a conflict is brewing, defer to your person. What are they asking for? Whom are they asking? Respect them as the expert and trust that eventually you will be the person called in to help.

At the same time, if you are empowering your person to do whatever it is that they need to do to cope with their loss, there is a chance that they might not ask you for help. How are you going to handle that?

Be Patient

When a delivery from the vegetarian restaurant down the street came on Day Five, I was confident I knew who had sent it. I texted "thank you" to my friend Mallory. She lived 12 hours away.

She responded instantly with, "I don't know how to be there for you without being there." I wrote back promising that I would need her later. I knew that was true on Day Five.

Since that moment, Mallory has followed my lead. She waited patiently until I was ready to call her onto the field. While she waited, she connected with some of Will's coworkers whom she knew closely. They showed up for each other, coordinated travel to the funeral together, listened to each other when they needed to share their feelings, and held each other tightly when they cried. When I told her the best resource that I'd found was Megan Devine's book, *It's OK That You're Not OK: Meeting Grief and Loss in a Culture That Doesn't Understand*, she bought herself a copy so she could understand too but without my having to explain it.

Then, after the funeral and Christmas, when everyone else had to go back to work, that's when I called on Mallory for help. She and her husband, Chris, came and stayed with me for a week. She willingly watched more TV than she ever had while sitting next to me on the couch. Chris fixed the drain in my bathtub. They made me dinner every night. They've let me come to their house for all-inclusive vacations where I sleep and read and they feed me.

Mallory could have given up in the early days of my grief because I didn't have a role for her, but she didn't. Instead, she sat in my front row and let me do what was best for me, which was letting other people be present with me in the earliest days of my life without Will. While she waited to help me, she led from the bench by learning what she could about my experience with grief, supporting others, and taking care of herself too.

It is a good thing that your person will have a team to help them and love them through this loss. You alone cannot do everything and be everything for them through the long haul of their grief. You won't last that way, no matter your skills or your capacity for self-care. If your support isn't being called on immediately, trust that it will be eventually. While you wait to be called on for your skills, continue to love your person unconditionally.

Welcome to the Team

Being a grief ally requires that you respect your person as the expert in what their grief feels like and that you remain curious about their very individual experience. Being a grief ally also demands that you empower your person to ask for what they need to cope, and if that means they need the skills and support of other people, you respect their decisions. You've committed to loving your person no matter what, right? Here's where you show you really can.

Grief allyship asks that you recognize and value the other people who want to help. Your person will have a variety of needs as they learn to live without their beloved, and having a team to help them meet those needs is a really great thing. With a team, your person can rely on a diversity of people and their strengths, which means being able to help in areas of your special skills rather than having to try to do everything. If you don't feel comfortable in a kitchen, you don't have to be there! Maybe, instead, what your person needs from you is your attention to detail when their brain isn't working? While you wait to be the one who is present in the moment when your skills and strengths are needed, be supportive of the team and respect your person's decisions and wishes when others are called upon for help.

While you wait, you can also work on building skills that you'll need in the future. Active listening will be a critical tool as time passes and as your person tries to make sense of the changes happening in their life because their beloved is no longer present. In the next chapter, I'll teach you how to be an excellent active listener.

Comfort and Ease: Ideas for How to Be a Grief Ally

- **Make connections with your teammates.**

    Connect with others who want to support your person. Start a group chat to centralize information and coordinate efforts. Check in with others to see how they're coping. Do they need someone they can trust to talk about what they're experiencing? Can you offer some peer support?

- **Centralize information about strengths and assets.**

    Build a spreadsheet to centralize information about who has which strengths, assets, or resources on your person's support team. Not everyone needs to be able to make food. My friend Martha is incredible at editing, and reviewed important text messages and emails that I needed to send. Others were willing to look after my cat if I wanted to go away. Think about what might be helpful to your person in the short term and long term. Does someone have a hot tub? Tuesday afternoons free to drop by and help with light housekeeping? Guest rooms available to your person across the country? Is there someone willing to cut your person's grass? Walk the dog? Take the kids out for a day?

- **Express your unconditional love.**

    Write your person a note reminding them of your unconditional love. Let them know that you want them to do whatever they have to do to survive the death of their beloved. They don't need your permission to do so, but having your support could mean a lot.

CHAPTER 5

LISTENING WITHOUT FIXING: THE ONE SKILL YOU NEED TO HAVE

I promise to listen, just listen.

An Echo in Validation

When the car we'd hired for the visitation pulled up outside of the funeral home, I was squished in the backseat between Gab and Sarah, two of my best friends. The driver asked if they should circle the block one more time before pulling into the driveway, but I declined. We rolled slowly up toward the door.

My heart was pounding, and my stomach knotted. I didn't want to go inside. In that building my beloved waited. Seeing his body would make it real that, between the two of us, there was only one heartbeat now. It'd be confirmed that I was alive and he was dead.

With my friends on either side of me, our clammy hands and elbows were interlocked, having woven a nest in the backseat of the car. I closed my eyes and took some deep breaths. Without a word, they inhaled and exhaled with me in unison.

My throat was lumpy and getting tighter by the second. I didn't want to do what was coming next. But I needed to find the courage to go inside.

"Grief is just love with no place to go," I said at a volume barely louder than a whisper.

My front row heard me. They echoed in validation, "Grief is just love with no place to go."

Listening: The No. 1 Skill You Need Right Now

As a grief ally, you're probably going to worry a lot about saying the right thing. Before we get to what's the right or wrong thing to say, let's focus on what's even more important to start. The single most valuable tool that a grief ally can have is being able to listen actively. You have the power to increase your person's chances of growing beyond the death of their beloved and having a meaningful life in the future—but to do that, you need to be able to be a safe and secure space for them to share what they're experiencing. Without that assurance, there's a risk that your person won't be able to tend to their grief in ways that they need to. What's more, suppressed emotions, if left unspoken and unheard, can cause secondary issues for your person, including physical illness. But when you are willing to witness their story and its details, possibly over and over and over, you can help your person make sense of what is happening and what has happened to the life that they knew.

In this chapter I'm going to teach you what active listening is, why it's different from simply listening, and how to do it effectively. I'll also cover some misconceptions about what good listening looks like. With these lessons, you'll be able to provide the kind of audience that your person needs to process all the changes that will happen in their life because of the death of their beloved.

Why Your Person Needs You to Listen

Storytelling is a longstanding therapeutic tool in bereavement. It's useful for making sense of what has happened and combating feelings of isolation. In one of the most well-known books about grief, *On Grief and Grieving*, authors Elizabeth Kübler-Ross and David Kessler write that "telling the story helps to dissipate the pain. Telling your story often and in detail is primal to the grieving process. You must get it out. Grief must be witnessed to be healed. Grief shared is grief abated."[18] They go on to share that storytelling can help to rebuild and recreate structure in one's life that has been lost because of one or multiple losses. But the power of storytelling is not exclusive to the sharing of experiences. As Kübler-Ross and Kessler put it: "Grief must be witnessed to be healed." So, the power of storytelling also lies in the listening, and that's where you can really help your person.

Your person is going to need people around them who are willing to listen, possibly for years, as they process what is going on in their life. They're going to have to make sense of and cope with not just the initial and primary loss of their beloved, but then all the secondary losses that unfold over time. Without safe and secure people around them who can listen, your person will carry their experiences and feelings in their brain and in their body. Such internalization is dangerous coping behavior. Holding onto painful emotions can cause trauma to the human body and manifest as depression, generalized anxiety, low self-esteem, etc.[19] Any or all of those reactions take a toll on your person's mental and physical health. And if that happens, it will only make their life even more difficult. But if you and others are capable and willing to listen, witness, and validate your person's feelings and experiences within their grief, you are giving them the best chance to move through this painful experience without carrying long-lasting emotional scars. You can create that safe and supportive environment for them by being able to actively listen.

What Is Active Listening?

Active listening is more complex than just hearing what someone is saying. It takes all of your attention and a lot of energy. It requires staying engaged in what your person is sharing, verbally and nonverbally. When you're actively listening, you're fully concentrating on what is being expressed and taking it in with all your senses. The person who is speaking has your undivided attention.

The opposite of active listening is as simple as not giving your person your undivided attention. Picking up your phone, looking out the window, or watching the TV in the midst of an intimate conversation doesn't convey that the environment is a safe space to share. It sends the opposite message that whatever your person is sharing isn't important enough for you to listen attentively. That message is invalidating to what your person is experiencing, and after they've mustered the courage to share their most vulnerable feelings with you, that can be a truly destructive experience for them.

If you've never been taught how to actively listen before,

try this exercise. Observe how you listen to others in the next conversation that you have. As the other person is speaking, pay attention to where your mind goes. Are you actually listening to what they're saying or is your mind jumping to how you're going to respond? Is that response something that you want to share about yourself? Are you offering unsolicited advice? Are you curious and asking more questions? Are there ideas waiting in the wings of your brain that you're ready to jump in with at the next break? All those tendencies are why active listening takes energy to be able to do it properly and practice to do it well. You'll notice quickly how your brain shifts its focus away from what the other person is saying if you're not intentional about keeping it focused on listening and observing the other person in the conversation. As an active listener, you're listening to learn and to understand—and that's it!

Active listening is at the core of all therapeutic relationships. With active listening, you can build the level of trust and respect that your person is going to need from you to be able to share their most vulnerable emotions and experiences. As you now know, social support systems hold incredible value in trauma recovery, but their value is not exclusive to just being in the presence of other supportive humans. In *The Body Keeps the Score*, Bessel Van der Kolk, writes that "[t]he critical issue is *reciprocity*: being truly heard and seen by the people around us, feeling that we are held in someone else's mind and heart."[20] If you can be with your person and show them that you are truly listening to what they're sharing then you're creating a safe space. That safe space is exactly what your person will need for their physiology to calm down so they can grow beyond the death of their beloved. So, let's teach you how to actively listen.

How to Actively Listen

Understanding what it means to be an active listener and why it's important is a great start. Next, it's time to actually learn how to do it.

It's important to keep in mind that active listening is a twofold practice. While actively listening, you are engaged in what your person is saying, verbally and through their body language. You're staying curious and looking for key ideas and feelings that they're expressing. On the outside, you're using verbal and nonverbal cues to signal to your person that you're paying attention and that you understand what they're expressing, using what is referred to as *immediacy behaviors*.

Immediacy behaviors are verbal and nonverbal behavioral cues that will send signals to your person that your attention is undivided. Verbal immediacy behaviors are the quick words and noises we use every day—you know, things like "yes," "mmhmm," "okay," "hmm," that indicate you're following the conversation and help to move it forward. Nonverbal immediacy behaviors include things like leaning toward the person who is speaking to you, letting your facial expressions reflect what's happening on their face (i.e., if they smile you can smile, if they're laughing you can laugh, if they're crying it's okay to cry too), and nodding your head as a cue that they can continue sharing.

As we covered before, the *only* goal of active listening is to validate your person's emotional experience. Megan Devine, author of *It's OK That You're Not OK*, says it best: "To feel truly comforted by someone, you need to feel heard in your pain. You need the reality of your loss reflected back to you—not diminished, not diluted. It seems counterintuitive, but true comfort in grief is acknowledging the pain, not in trying to make it go away."[21]

As the conversation moves forward, stay curious about your person's experience. Periodically paraphrasing what your person is saying is called tracking, and it's another way to signal that you're giving them your full attention. Best practice is to follow tracking with a "checkout," which is a question like, "Did I get that right?" or "Is that what you mean?"

You should also know that you don't have to be physically in the same room with your person to be able to actively listen successfully. An article published in the *Western Journal of Communication* by Graham D. Bodie and colleagues (2015) studied the effectiveness of the immediacy behaviors that make up active listening.[22] The study results found that when the listener used eye-contact, paraphrasing, and asking open-ended questions the talker perceived them as more emotionally aware, and the talker felt better. The study also compared the effectiveness of verbal and nonverbal listening behaviors and found that the verbal behaviors (sounds and words like "mmhmm," "okay," "yes," "oh, tell me more," etc.) were *three times* as likely as nonverbal behaviors to produce this outcome. Those conclusions mean that you can provide effective support–even *more* effective, in fact–to your person by actively listening to them over the phone or via video.

How to Get Started

If active listening is a new concept for you, it's important to remember that it takes time and practice to master. To help you get started, below are verbal suggestions you can use to validate your person's experience throughout a conversation, as well as to signal that you are listening attentively.

Validating your person and making sure that they feel heard can *sound* like:

- Repeating exactly what your person has said.
- "Do you want to tell me more about that?"
- "That sounds so painful/conflicting/hurtful." (Or insert whatever other feeling it sounds like.)
- "I'm sorry you're feeling that way right now."
- "That makes so much sense."
- "I'm here to listen."
- "You are right."
- "I believe you."
- "I understand why you feel that way."
- "Thank you for trusting me enough to share that."

Nonverbal signals to validate and make sure your person feels heard can *look* like:

- Nodding in agreement
- High fives
- Hand on your chest
- Hand on their shoulder [with permission]
- Holding their hand [with permission]

It's worth noting that some people are quite introverted and find verbal conversations difficult sometimes, especially when there are difficult emotions involved. I know that can be the case for me as an introverted millennial, because when I'm talking to someone versus typing to them, I don't get the time I like to prepare what I want to say. Being able to think about what I want to say has made text messaging conversations the most comfortable space for me to express myself honestly. I share this insight with you because your person might be the same, and it's important to know what is their preferred method of conversation.

At the end of the day, you may end up actively listening to them through words on screens, but the same instructions apply. You can use immediacy behaviors that are words, emojis, or GIFs to show that you are listening, and you can use tracking and checkout questions to confirm your full attention. Whatever the medium is that you and your person are using to communicate, it's possible to actively listen there.

Active Listening Does Not Include These Behaviors

Grief allyship is challenging work because sometimes the lines between your person's thoughts and feelings can blur with your own if you're not conscious of how you're showing up as a grief ally. In my opinion, these blur traps are most likely to happen in conversations when you feel like you have the answer to your person's problems, when you can relate to what they're experiencing, or when you're shocked by their honesty. Each of these scenarios has negative consequences for your person. Because of that potential, I've listed some examples of what is *not* active listening that you can use as a guide to avoid undue harm to your person.

Active Listening Is Not Silence

If you're opening a conversation, be prepared to engage. Once your person has shared their truth with you after being invited to do so, if you then give them nothing back but silence, you're sending the message that what they've shared is too much for you. Silence can feel like rejection.[23] Silence can also encourage your person to retract inward, believing that their emotions aren't okay to share.

Once silence is interpreted as rejection, it's not uncommon for individuals to begin keeping their feelings to themselves to maintain social norms. Such withdrawal is a problem because people who don't give space to their darkest emotions, or who judge those feelings in themselves too harshly, can end up feeling even more psychologically stressed.[24] Chronic stress can affect both our physical and psychological well-being by causing a variety of problems, which include anxiety, insomnia, muscle pain, high blood pressure, and a weakened immune system. Over time, these issues can contribute to the development of major illnesses such as heart disease and depression.[25] For brains that are still developing, repeated rejection has the power to build entrenched beliefs that there is something fundamentally wrong with showing big or negative emotions. These beliefs build defenses in the brain that suppress these emotions altogether, which will also cause psychological stress and lead to the symptoms I've mentioned above.[26] Long story short: There are consequences to silence.

Instead of scrambling for the "right" words, what you have to remember is that your role here isn't to do anything more than listen and validate what your person is experiencing. They don't need the "right words." All your person needs to hear from you is, "I'm here and I'm listening. Do you want to tell me more?"

Which brings us to…

Active Listening Is Not Problem-Solving

In Chapter 2, you learned that some people are more likely to express their grief as problems rather than feelings. Doka and Martin in *Grieving Beyond Gender* term these individuals as instrumental grievers.[27] If your person is expressing problems, you'll probably find that solutions swirl around in your mind. That's okay and normal when someone is sharing their discomfort with you. As an outsider, it might seem like their hardship could be easily avoided, and because you love your person as much as you do, you'll want to help take away the pain. Unfortunately, problem-solving without permission sends the message that you're not willing and able to see them in their truth. If you jump straight to problem-solving, your person might interpret your response as not having the patience to validate what they're experiencing, which again, can feel like rejection.

If you really feel that what your person needs to hear is *your* solution to their problem, ask permission first. That approach can sound like, "Would you be open to my trying to solve this problem with you?" If you've been following the steps that I've laid out in the book so far, your person will hopefully feel confident enough to give you their honest answer.

Active Listening Is Not Saying "Me Too"

This one is tough because we're often told that sharing stories is supposed to make us feel less alone. Sure, there will be a time and place in your person's grief to do that, but in the early days it's best to keep stories about your own grief to yourself (or find someone else besides your person with whom you can share them if needed). Saying "me too" shifts the focus of the conversation away from supporting your person and onto you, to supporting you and your pain, or to establishing you as the expert in whatever they're experiencing. The latter will quickly send you down the slippery slope of problem-solving, and I've already shared why that's not helpful.

The exception to that rule would be that if you feel that your lived experience will help your person to know that you're listening or that you truly understand what they're feeling. If yes, share your story. But my advice would be to use your experience in the context of tracking the conversation and then checking out with a question. You might try saying something like:

> "I think I understand what you're saying about how it feels like something is missing when you go to places that were special to the two of you. Since my dad died, I've felt like there's an empty space in all our new family photos even if there isn't actually a visible space. Is that what it feels like for you?"

Using your own experience in the context of tracking and checkouts in the conversation keeps the focus on your person. That connection is what they need in the early period of their grief. They need to see, hear, and feel their reality reflected and validated.

Being able to listen to your person's experience of grief and loss without implying rejection, without jumping to problem-solving, and without making the conversation about you, reinforces to your person that you are on their team. If you can do that, you're proving to them that you do in fact love them in any state, including the messiest ones, and that you are willing to sit with them in their pain.

Take Your Time

Your person might not want to talk with you about what they're experiencing and that's okay. They may only be capable of menial conversation in the early days of their grief, but that mode doesn't mean that your value as a listener is any less important.

My two longest friendships are with Katelyn and Sarah. We became friends in elementary school and always called ourselves the tripod because, well, there are three of us. Now, though, we all live in different parts of the country, so they couldn't be with me immediately after Will died. Instead, Katelyn, Sarah, and their partners sent me a gift basket of fruit and cheese on the day that I told them Will was dead.

Did I need a basket of fruit and cheese on the day after Will died? No, probably not.

Did they feel helpless in the moment and feel compelled to do something for me? Yes. And culturally, what are we told to do? Send food.

I knew that not being there physically with me was challenging for both of them. I tried to keep them updated, and they continued to check in, but I wasn't really sharing much. On Friday night, I sat in my bathtub and ate some of the grapes from the basket. They were good grapes, so I told them so via text message.

"These are really good grapes," I said.

"I'm happy they're good grapes." replied Sarah.

"What color are they?" asked Katelyn.

"Red," I answered.

"Seedless?"

"Yep."

"Mmm."

This conversation about grapes went on for about 10 minutes.

I didn't think anything of it until months later when I was talking with Sarah and mentioned how people like me need the people around us just to listen in the beginning. She responded with, "Yeah, like the grapes."

I didn't know what she meant, so she explained.

"When you started to text me about grapes," she said, "I freaked out. I told Marlee [Sarah's wife], I don't care about the grapes. I can do more than that! Why isn't she asking for my help?"

Marlee told her, with love and compassion, "Maybe she just wants to talk about grapes and that's enough to be helpful right now." Marlee was right. At that moment, I really just needed to talk about the grapes.

Actively Listen, and Then Keep on Listening

Being witnessed and heard by others will help your person make sense of their world again. Your person will shift and change as they process their losses, so it's important to remember that your only goal is to stay engaged in the conversation. You don't need to hold them to any plans, beliefs, or feelings. Be a safe space for them to explore what's going on inside of them. Just actively listen and then keep on listening.

I understand, though, that for you to be able to actively listen, a conversation needs to be started, and it's tough to know what to say to someone whose beloved has died. That's why I'm going to teach you what *not* to say (as well as, in many cases, what to say instead) in the next chapter.

Comfort and Ease: Ideas for How to Be a Grief Ally

- **Practice your new listening skills.**

    Practice active listening with other people. Use the lessons that I've taught you here to build your active listening skills. While others are speaking to you, exercise your listening muscles by giving them your undivided attention and validating what they are saying. Even better, ask someone else on your person's team to practice with you.

- **Get comfortable with silence.**

    Don't try to fill all the quiet moments in a conversation, but try to offer some affirming signal to avoid long periods of silence. Pauses are natural in conversation, and if there's a pause, experiment with letting your person be the one to break it. A conversation does not have to be full of words the entire time to be meaningful or cathartic.

- **Build a toolkit for feeling different emotions.**

    Assemble a bundle of items to soothe the variety of emotions your person will experience in their grief: Tissues and a soft playlist for when they're sad. Or maybe rock music and a pillow to scream into when they're angry, or even a hammer to smash things with. Get creative with it.

CHAPTER 6

POETRY, CLICHÉS, AND NONSENSE: WHAT NOT TO SAY

I promise to skip the clichés and ask questions when I don't know what to say.

Moving On Isn't an Option

Nine months after Will died, I had some questions about the practices of the Catholic faith with regard to spreading ashes. Not being Catholic myself, I only knew one expert who could give me a clear answer. So, I found the courage to call the priest who had led all of Will's funeral ceremonies.

"Hi, Aly," he said on the phone. "Of course, I remember you. How can I help you?"

I felt relieved. I wouldn't have to explain who I was, that Will was dead, and why I was calling him specifically to answer my question.

"I have a question I'm hoping you can help me with," I said, reciting the script I'd planned out in my head.

He said he'd do his best to help. I took a breath, calling all my courage to the tip of my tongue.

"In Catholicism, is there a time limit on when ashes should be spread after someone has been cremated?" I said in one quick breath like I was blowing out a candle.

"Okay, well, no. But as Catholics we don't spread ashes."

I should have been inhaling by this point, but I held my breath. I had entered this conversation seeking a yes or no answer. Now I was getting more information than I was prepared for. He continued on, sharing what happens in Catholic traditions. I braced myself for the intensity of hot and cold sensations that were rising from my knees and falling from the top of my head simultaneously.

"Does that answer your question?"

"Um, yeah, I guess so," I muttered with all my muscles clenched.

"You sound conflicted," He observed, as if he could see through the phone and was watching me trying to keep my body upright with my kitchen counter.

"I am," I said, trying to keep my composure while monitoring an overwhelming urge to vomit. Then, without pause, he violated three fundamentals of grief allyship with one sentence.

"Aly, maybe it's time for you to move on, to start a new chapter."

I've experienced some really ignorant and hurtful statements since Will's death, including being called a "selfish f--king c--t" by one of Will's close friends, but this one hurt because I trusted the priest. I let him in and believed he was an ally. But this was not grief allyship. Grief allies don't try to fix anyone's grief or problem-solve without permission or believe that moving on is possible when someone's beloved dies.

Suggesting that I move on was ignorant and dismissive. Being told to move on suggests that I would be capable of leaving Will in the past, of silently rejecting all the love that suddenly had nowhere to go and the pain I've endured as I've slowly watched my life come apart at the seams because pieces of it can't be sustained without Will's presence.

By his suggesting that I move on, I'm sure that the priest was simply trying to be helpful—albeit, causing the opposite effect. His words simply told me that he was no longer a safe person to share my grief with, and I haven't since.

Why You Should Skip Clichés

There's a lot of unhelpful or harmful shit that gets said after a death. While the intention behind what's said is meant to be kind and helpful, virtually all the clichés fall short in their impact and will leave your person confused, shamed, or feeling dismissed. Your person doesn't need any of that on top of their grief, which is already stressful. Saying the wrong thing will add to that stress, and worse, you might send the message to your person that you are not willing to sit with them and their pain. Conversely, when you can say the right thing or be courageous enough to ask questions when you're uncertain not only will you help your person in that moment but also reinforce that you are truly a grief ally.

To save you from some trial and error, I've highlighted some common phrases and clichés in this chapter that are mistakenly used in grief support and have broken down why they can be damaging. I've also offered some advice about what you can say that will be helpful and even comforting to your person. I can't promise you that you won't make mistakes, but with this advice you'll understand why the words you use will matter to your person.

"How Are You?" Is a Loaded Question

Living with grief is emotionally exhausting. Your person could be feeling a million emotions a day and often many all at the same time. Life can feel like a roller coaster. It's very difficult to put that into words. "How are you?" is not an easy question to answer. Here's my advice: When you're feeling like "how are you?" is what you want to say to your person, check in with yourself before you ask it. Do you have the time and energy to be present with however they are feeling right now? Or are you just thinking about your person and want them to know? If it's the latter, make a statement instead of asking a question. You might try the following approaches:

- "Hey, I love you."
- <a heart emoji>
- "Thinking about you."
- <a hug emoji>
- A GIF that conveys the message you're trying to send

If you're hoping to open a conversation with your person because you have the time and energy to be with them in that moment, why not start with the basics? Ask a more specific question like:

- Hi, I'm free for a little bit. Want to talk?
- How are you at this moment?
- Would you like some company right now?
- Has anything felt good today?
- Were you able to get some sleep last night?
- Have you been able to eat today?
- How is your tissue supply?

Mallory got into the habit early on of simply texting me "Hi." It's nothing fancy or elaborate, but every time she sends the text, it's a signal to me that she has a moment, and if I want to talk the floor is mine. Sometimes I take it. I'll rhyme off all the things I've felt since the last time we talked. Everything that has made me sad, angry, exhausted, or excited. Other times I won't respond at all, and she has promised me that my silence doesn't hurt her feelings.

Bottom line here: *Why* are you asking "how are you?" Find the answer to that question for yourself and then act accordingly.

Skip the Silver Linings

The phrase "at least" gets thrown around a lot in discussions with the bereaved about grief.

At least you got five good years with him.

At least they had life insurance.

At least they're not suffering anymore.

At least they're at peace now.

I understand that the clear intention behind using the phrase *at least* is to provide comfort, but the message it carries doesn't feel good for the recipient because there's a silent but implied second half of the sentence. Megan Devine shares this effect in her book *It's OK That You're Not OK,* calling the missing half of the sentence the ghost sentence.[28] That ghost sentence is asking your person to diminish their pain in favor of something more positive. Asking your person to dismiss their pain is not grief allyship. An ally is willing to sit with their person and their pain.

To avoid this "silver lining" mistake, Devine offers a helpful exercise. For each of the above "at least" sentences, add the second half of the sentence that's being implied: "…so stop feeling so bad."

At least you got five good years with him…so stop feeling so bad.

At least they had life insurance…so stop feeling so bad.

At least they're not suffering anymore…so stop feeling so bad.

At least they're at peace now…so stop feeling so bad.

Pretty powerful stuff, right? With this exercise, it's easy to quickly pick up on why it's not helpful to insert a positive spin on any of your person's pain. Try to catch yourself before you use "at least" because if you do—whether it's your intention or not—you're not allowing your person the space to express their truth. Instead, you're effectively minimizing or even dismissing their feelings, either of which is unhelpful and possibly harmful to their well-being.

Gratitude Won't Take Away Anyone's Pain

Similar to using the phrase "at least," it's not uncommon to encourage someone to be grateful for what they had while they had it. The intention here seems to be to try to help a bereaved person to focus less on their loss. Again, the message is dismissive. The reality and truth of your person's experience is that this experience hurts. Asking them to focus on gratitude rather than their sadness invalidates their emotions.

In my case, I am both grateful that I had Will in my life for as long as I did and am allowed to be deeply sad and angry that he isn't here anymore. Your person is entitled to their own complex feelings about their loss, whatever those may be.

Keep Your Hope for the Future to Yourself

Hope comes from a kind place, so you might be tempted to encourage your person to look forward to things in the future to cheer them up or discourage them from being sad. Unfortunately for someone who has just experienced the death of their beloved, the idea can feel like a lot of pressure when too many people suggest what their hopes are for your person's future. Expressing too much hope can also feel dismissive and invalidating to your person, inferring that you would prefer to see them in a more positive state rather than respecting what state they're in right now.

It's possible that your person's grief will be marked with hopelessness for a while. It's common to feel hopeless if the death was unexpected, out-of-order, or tragic. Being forced to look toward a future that doesn't have their beloved in it can be debilitating. I know you want your person to be okay. It's only natural to hope that they will be okay. But until they're ready for it, keep your hope to yourself and just be present with them and what they're experiencing moment to moment. On the topic of hope, grief expert and author David Kessler, in his book *Finding Meaning*, suggests saying that "Until you can find it, I'll hold it for you."[29]

Not Everything Happens for a Reason

"Everything happens for a reason" gets thrown around a lot too, but just because it's popular doesn't mean it's true. Sometimes I wonder if people use it just to tie a nice little bow around circumstances that our brains can't reconcile. The truth is that not everything happens for a reason. Experiencing the death of a loved one doesn't have to be a lesson. Having to figure out a Plan B because your Plan A fell from a cliff doesn't have to be a lesson. Some things are explainable, but not everything. People die at random—not because they're special or chosen or because they were supposed to die. Do your best to stay away from catch-all phrases if you are grappling with something you can't explain.

They'll Get Different, Not Better

As your person adjusts to living with grief, it'll be tempting to be excited about their acclimatization. Your reaction stems from signs of things that look and sound similar to who they were before their beloved's death. You might be tempted to say things like:

- "You sound better."
- "You sound like yourself again."
- "You're looking happy again."

Your person will never be the person that they were before their beloved died. Grief isn't an illness from which to recover. Something fundamental to the fabric of their being will be different forever more. A good life might grow around their grief, but it won't be the same life as before. They'll probably find a new equilibrium, but that doesn't mean they're *better*. What they are now is different.

Remember That the Opposite of Strength Is Weakness

Complimenting people on what they're doing well is a pretty common human practice. Holding it together and looking "strong" isn't something to compliment about someone when they are grieving, though. Glorifying "strength" during loss sends the message that the messier, snottier, teary-eye states of grief are "weakness" and are less appropriate. You'll be running the risk of sending the message that those expressions aren't okay and should be suppressed, or that if your person's grief is "messy" that they're doing grief wrong. None of those assumptions are correct, and I know that you know that now. Just let your person survive and love them in whatever state they are in.

Most human beings are resilient at their core. One day, your person will likely be able to carry the weight of their grief. They'll carry it invisibly, and to any stranger they meet, they'll make it look like it never happened. But resilience takes time. The muscles they'll need to carry their grief will not appear overnight. Give them time to build their strength rather than encouraging them to "stay strong."

Your Person's Grief Does Not Have to Become a Story of Epic Transformation

We often glorify the individuals who do "extraordinary" things after extreme hardship. The people who lose limbs and then run marathons, the bereaved parents who start charities, and the widows who write books, among other accomplishments, but we really shouldn't. Glorifying the individuals who grieve by doing things and problem-solving has the effect of comparing their experience with the people who just manage to survive their experience with grief, and that isn't fair. No one's experience of grief is the same.

What your person has experienced does not have to become a story of epic transformation. They do not have to *come back* from this loss as a better, faster, stronger version of themselves. Your person was great enough before their beloved died. If they can survive in a world without someone they love dearly, that is a win. That's all the pressure they should have to endure.

In *It's OK that You're Not OK*, Megan Devine writes that "[w]hen someone else ascribes growth or meaning to your loss, it diminishes your power, gives subtle shaming or judgment to who you were before, and tells you that you needed this somehow."[30] Keep in mind that your person was great enough before their beloved died. They are still great in whatever state they are in now. And they will be great enough in their future no matter what it looks like.

No One but Your Person Is the Boss of Their Grief

Some people think they're being helpful when they use someone's beloved to suggest how one ought to be carrying on with life. They'll make statements that sound like:

"[Your beloved] wouldn't want you to be sad."
"[Your beloved] would want you to find love again."
"[Your beloved] would want you to get out of bed."
"[Your beloved] would want you to take care of yourself."

Sure, it can be comforting to think of your person's beloved and how they'd like your person to live life without them, but letting anyone other than your person define how they live with their grief isn't helpful. In particular, letting someone who is dead (meaning they can't be debated) define how your person ought to live with grief can set them up for failure. As we've covered in previous chapters, the only *right way* to live with the pain of their loss is the way that feels best to them. No one else should have the right to define what that looks like—not even the person they lost.

Each of the above statements gives the impression that your person should stop feeling what they're feeling. The meaning can also come across like you know your person's beloved better than they do. No one can settle that fight, so don't have it.

The Exception to Every Rule

Your person is the leader here, and you are a front-row student. That mindset should trump all of the rules that I've listed elsewhere. If your person is using language that I've advised you not to use, believe your person, not me. As you watch, listen, and learn from your person about what their grief looks and feels like, what brings them comfort, and what makes their life easier, believe that it is their truth in that moment. You are allowed to use the language that they are using. If your person wants their grief to epically transform them or they want to make their beloved the boss of their grief or they want to use gratitude to cope, they are allowed to do that. Take your cue from them. Do not forget, though, that grief is dynamic, and your person is allowed to and will change their mind about what language feels good to them. So, with that, respect them if and when their preferences change too.

You Can Talk About Their Beloved

I haven't said "don't talk about their beloved" on purpose. You should absolutely talk about their beloved. I've read that people stop talking about people who have died because they're afraid that they'll remind those who are still living of something that they'd rather forget. That assumption couldn't be more wrong. Sharing conversation about their beloved might be exactly what your person wants.

In his book, *The Other Side of Sadness: What the New Science of Bereavement Tells Us About Life After Loss,* George A. Bonanno, author and professor of clinical psychology at Columbia University, writes:

> "We are not accustomed to thinking of grief as a process of finding comfort. The idea seems a bit odd, but this is precisely what resilient people tend to do. Regardless of what the relationship was actually like, resilient people are generally better able to gain a feeling of comfort from remembering the relationship during bereavement. They are also more likely to find comfort in talking about or thinking about the deceased, which, they report, makes them feel happy or at peace."[31]

All I ever think about is Will. All I ever want to think about is Will. I felt oddly good at each of Will's funerals because all we did was talk about him. He was my favorite person on the planet. It's my greatest fear that people will stop talking about him.

If you're unsure if your person wants to talk about their beloved, a great gift you can give to them is to ask if they'd like to and to respect the answer that they give you.

Near the three-month mark after Will's death, I felt the support that I had up until that point starting to settle. People had other things to do and to take care of. I understood that. There had been a number of offers to reach out whenever I needed something, but I never responded because I didn't need anything tangible. But as the mood in my community was shifting, there was something I needed and wanted everyone to know. So, I made a statement on Facebook:

> I've read that people get scared about reaching out. They worry about what to say or fear saying the wrong thing. And all of that comes from the belief that whatever you say should make things better or the pain more bearable for me.
>
> I don't need you to do any of that or be that for me. I'm not expecting it from you.
>
> If you're worried that you'll remind me of something I'd rather forget, be assured that I'm never going to forget about Will.
>
> If you want someone to reminisce with, I would really love it if you chose me to be that person from time to time. If you're thinking about Will, I'd love to know. Telling stories, sharing photos or videos about him are like gold to me.

The Saturday night following this post, I was at a party. The guests were a small contingent of a larger group that were supposed to be at an annual banquet for an organization that Will volunteered for. At the last minute, it was called off because COVID-19 was rapidly spreading and shutting down the world, so a small group of us got together. As I was leaving the party, I put on my jacket and shoes and I stepped outside, waiting for the friends I was going to walk home with. The noise inside disappeared when I closed the door, and when I turned around there were two young guys standing in the driveway, next to the door.

"Hey, Aly."

"Oh! Hey," I said, a bit startled.

They watched me, seeming to expect me to keep walking down the driveway, but I just stood there. "I'm waiting for Nick and Carlie. They're coming with me," I explained.

They nodded, and then we all stood there in silence.

I'd had just enough to drink to add, "Well, this is a bit awkward" to the muted conversation.

One of them was the host of the party, and he piped up then. "Can I, um, talk to you for a second?"

I followed him back inside and into his bedroom, which was right next to the front door. We sat down on his bed, and he opened his laptop. "I saw your post on Facebook," he said.

"Oh yeah?"

"Yeah," he said, "and the first time I read it I was like, 'Wow, this is definitely a cry for attention.'"

"Oh," I said with a laugh. I knew some people were going to interpret it that way.

"Yeah," he went on, "but then I read it again and, um, I really appreciated it."

He went on to tell me that he thought about Will all the time.

I smiled, my eyes welling up with tears.

This 23-year-old, who'd also lost a good friend, and I sat in his bedroom for 45 minutes laughing and crying together as we swapped stories, photos, and videos with Will in them. My friends walked home without me, but I walked home the happiest I'd been since Will had died.

When You Don't Know What to Say, Ask

At the end of the day, you love your person and you want to do what is best for them. If you're talking to them, ask what they need at that moment. It can be like a breath of fresh air when everyone is talking around what they're experiencing and not actually about it.

After Will died, I got a message from someone he'd worked with three years ago. Someone whom he'd known really well and whom we'd spent time with before we'd moved to separate coasts. He checked in, and we shared some lighthearted conversation. When the conversation seemed to stall in pleasantries, he said, "I'm sorry, Aly. Sometimes I struggle with knowing what is right to say to you and whether I should ask about your life or just be a light distraction. I just want to be respectful." I can't tell you how good it felt to hear that someone was willing to ask about what was really going on rather than just checking in to check in so that they could check out again.

My friend Katie did the same thing around the anniversary of mine and Will's relationship. We were walking together and she said, "I was thinking that I should have wished you a happy anniversary yesterday. Would that have been okay? Is there another way I can acknowledge the date for you?" Because Katie asked, we were able to have an honest conversation about how to best recognize the bittersweet dates that I'm going to have for the rest of my life.

Your person might not know what they want or don't want to hear. If that's the case, the truth is always a great place to start. And if you make a mistake, know that, if you are willing, you can recover from it. I'm going to teach you how in the next chapter.

Comfort and Ease: Ideas for How to Be a Grief Ally

- **Be mindful of anniversaries, birthdays, significant dates, and holidays.**

    Special dates can be triggering. Before they arrive, bring them up in conversation with your person. Ask if they want to recognize them, celebrate them, ignore them, or something entirely different. Ask how you can be helpful on those dates. But also be mindful that if it's the first time they're experiencing them without their beloved they won't know how it's going to feel. Moreover, as time passes, their feelings about these special dates might change.

- **Share stories about their beloved.**

    During the ceremonies that mark a death a lot of stories are shared. These stories bring comfort to those who are listening, either reminding them of vivacious moments or keeping the person who has died alive and growing in their mind if they've never heard the story before. A great gift to your person might be to capture these stories. Write them down. Tell them in an audio note. Send a photo with a quick note about when and why it was taken.

- **Keep their beloved's memory alive.**

    Keep memories and traditions of their beloved alive if your person is okay with that. Keep going to restaurants that their beloved enjoyed. Drink the beer they liked. Contribute to causes they believed in. Visit places that were meaningful to them. Do push-ups on their beloved's birthday or something that they would have loved to do.

- **Help them find distractions or methods to take breaks from their grief.**

  It's okay and normal for your person to take breaks from actively grieving. If your person is interested in a specific activity that takes their mind off their loss for periods of time, take an interest in that activity, or if they're open to it, help them find an activity that feels good to them. Those activities could be creating art, playing video games, reading books, playing with Legos, woodworking, gardening, or tasks that they have to do (cooking, cleaning, working, etc.). This back and forth between actively experiencing grief and participating in restorative activities is called the Dual Process Model of Coping with Bereavement.[32]

CHAPTER 7

YOU'RE GOING TO MAKE MISTAKES: THIS IS HOW TO RECOVER

I promise to remain your ally even when I make mistakes.

You're Not Going to Be an A+ Student Instantly

Because everyone's experience with grief is unique, no one will be able to show up to help their person and be an A+ student at the beginning. Unfortunately, that shortfall means you're probably going to make a few mistakes while both you and your person get acquainted with what their particular brand of grief looks and feels like. On top of that, your person could be shifting and changing in their grief for some time. If that happens, you will have to shift and change how you support them as well. To be able to offer your person your allyship through the long haul of their grief, you need to be able to recover and ultimately learn from your mistakes.

From this chapter, I want you to understand that perfection isn't what you should strive for as a grief ally. Instead, I want you to believe that if you are making mistakes, then you are doing things right. This mindset shift will help you make space for all the learning that both you and your person have to do as their grief shifts and changes. This chapter also lays out a few simple steps for how to recover from mistakes and vulnerable moments that you have with your person, which includes how to make a great apology if you have to make one. With these tools, on top of what you've already learned in this book, you're going to be ready to stick around for the long haul of grief with your person. That's what great grief allies do: They remain committed even when things don't go as planned because they know that perfect doesn't exist in this role.

Grief Allies Can't Be Perfect

It's my understanding that a lot of the nervousness and apprehension about showing up for someone and their grief is the concern that you'll do something wrong, make a mistake, say the wrong thing—in short, that you won't be perfect. I'd like you to leave your desire for perfection out of your grief allyship. Perfectionism isn't possible here (or anywhere, really) and if you're striving for it, you're not only going to be less helpful to your person, but you're also limiting yourself and your ability to connect with others.

Perfection is about perception. It's an addictive belief system, and at its core, it leads us to believe that we're not good enough to simply be who we are as unique human beings. Seeking perfection puts our worthiness in the hands of others to judge us because we're seeking the approval of others. We believe that if we're perfect, we'll avoid judgment or shame from them. But perfection actually sets us up to feel shame or judgment, because when we end up being imperfect (since humans are not capable of perfection) we dig ourselves deeper into the belief that if we had just worked harder or knew better, we would have escaped these feelings of "not good enough." This thinking perpetuates an addictive cycle of continuing to try harder to be perfect, then never being perfect, and ultimately feeling that we are never enough.

We strive for perfection because admitting that we're not perfect would be exposing our vulnerabilities. And it's not uncommon to have been shamed for sharing your vulnerabilities in the past. Shame isn't something we're born with; rather, it's a physical and psychological response to being rejected by others after we've tried to connect with them by sharing our vulnerabilities.[33] To cope with shame and our feelings of not being good enough, we develop defenses (thoughts, emotions, and behaviors) to protect ourselves. We usually start building these defenses as children and carry them with us as we grow up.

These defenses—the thoughts, emotions, and behaviors that you're accustomed to using to protect yourself from uncomfortable emotions—are what Brené Brown, author, shame and vulnerability researcher, and renowned speaker calls "armor."[34] We all have armor. What kind of armor we're wearing, whether it's cardboard or metal or Kevlar—or something in between—has a lot to do with whether the environments that we grew up in felt safe enough as spaces to explore, learn, and express who we truly are. For some, lowering your armor is scary but manageable. For others, it feels impossible. Wherever you fall on the manageable-to-impossible scale is okay, but as Brené Brown's research has determined, our armor can prevent us from making meaningful connections and feeling like we belong, one of our innate human desires.

I'm not asking you to compromise your emotional safety to be an ally to your person by putting your armor down completely. But please know that you're not alone if you're feeling vulnerable and exposed in your grief support role. It's possible to feel that way even if you've lowered your armor only slightly.

In the role of grief support, your vulnerabilities are likely some variation of the following:

- You have absolutely no experience in supporting someone who is grieving
- you have no idea what the hell you're doing
- you're afraid you're going to do something wrong
- And/or you're terrified that if you don't do this *right*, you're going to lose your person

I know it's scary to admit you're vulnerable. I know that it doesn't feel good when we don't get things right. But I'm hoping that I can help a little with that impression at least in the context of grief support. It starts with a subtle mindset shift. Instead of thinking that if you're not making mistakes then you're getting grief allyship right, I want you to adopt the mindset that *if you are making mistakes, then you are doing grief support right.*

Making Mistakes Is More Than Okay

There isn't an easy way to break this to you, so brace yourself: To learn how to be exactly the kind of ally that your person needs in their grief, you're going to have to be all-in and completely present to what they're experiencing. You're going to have to sit in the front row and risk putting up your hand, even when you don't know the answer. To be fair, your person might not know the answer either. Figuring out what they'll need as their grief shapeshifts and transforms over time is going to take incredible courage, exploration, and experimentation from the both of you. The good news, though, is that with experimentation you and your person will both learn what feels good and what doesn't.

With the tools I've given you in this book, you will be in the best possible position to make educated guesses, as well as have the skill to ask questions when necessary. But because every person is unique and so is their grief, I can't give you more than that help. You and your person will have to figure out the rest on your own. Given the circumstances, you're probably going to make a few mistakes. You need to know that making mistakes is more than okay.

We all make mistakes when we're learning, no matter how compassionate, kind, or generous we are. The important thing is that when you make those mistakes, you don't throw up your hands and walk away completely. You love your person unconditionally. In this context, unconditionally means regardless of the mistakes that happen through the long haul of grief. So, instead of not being all-in because you're afraid of making mistakes, I want you to do the opposite. Be all-in and make mistakes. Let the love you have for your person trump all your fear and worry. Make the mistakes and then learn from them. That's how you'll become a great grief ally.

How to Keep Showing Up

In order to acknowledge mistakes and keep showing up for your person, you're going to need a recovery system. Following are my four suggested steps to help you take care of the discomfort that arises when you've made a mistake and how to effectively apologize if it's necessary. Ultimately, these steps will let your person know that you care deeply about being an ally to them in their grief. What's more, if you follow my advice, I believe that you can build a deeper connection between you and your person than you ever had before.

Step One: Get off the shame and blame emotional rollercoaster as soon as possible.

When you make a mistake you could experience feelings of embarrassment, guilt, humiliation, shame, or another kind of uncomfortable emotion. None of those reactions are uncommon, but if left unchecked they might send you off on a rollercoaster ride with beliefs that you're not capable, that you're a failure, or that you're not good enough to be able to support your person. None of those beliefs are true. Everyone is capable of supporting someone they love through the long haul of grief. The people who are great at it are the people who are courageous enough to keep showing up even when they make mistakes. As soon as you possibly can, throw the brakes on that runaway coaster.

There are a couple of ways that you can stop the shame and blame rollercoaster. I've listed two options below that you can use independently or together. Choose what feels right for you and then move on to Step Two.

Option 1:

Brené Brown has famously said that shame can't live in a vacuum. If you can, tell someone how you're feeling—someone you trust who can sit and empathize with you. To decide who that person should be, revisit the Ring Theory from Chapter 3 and find someone in your community who is further from the epicenter of this death than you are, someone who can actively listen. If you don't have someone to talk to, you can also talk to yourself. You might try writing to yourself in a journal, pacing the floor, verbalizing the events of what happened, or ranting into a voice note on your phone. All of them can be helpful!

Option 2:

When I make mistakes, my rollercoaster often takes the shape of replaying the event over and over in my mind. What I've found helpful to stop the replays is to create an affirmation that gives me permission to feel the way I'm feeling and reminds me why I took the risk in the first place.

For example, once upon a time I had a crush on a boy. Instead of waiting around trying to interpret subtle signals of whether or not he might like me back, I told him, straight up, that I liked him. He told me, straight up, that he did not feel the same way. Was this interaction embarrassing for me? Definitely. Do I still play it over in my head sometimes? Yes, unfortunately. But when my brain starts replaying that interaction, I say to myself, "Clarity is kind." And I repeat it as many times as possible. *Clarity is kind, Clarity is kind, Clarity is kind.* Until I believe it again. To me, there was a reason I was vulnerable. I wanted to know if this person liked me back. Getting the answer from them, even though it ended up being "no" was my getting what I needed. Getting my needs met is how I show kindness to myself. *Clarity is kind.*

You can create your own affirmation to calm your brain when it starts to replay your vulnerable grief ally moments. My advice is to keep it short and meaningful. Consider something like:

I am showing up because I love my person.

I am here to learn and not to be perfect.

Mistakes happen when I'm learning and that's okay.

I am worthy of love and connection no matter what.

Repeat your affirmation as many times as necessary. Notice what you feel in your body as you repeat it. If there was tension, does it ease up as you repeat your affirmation? Your affirmation should have some effect. If it doesn't, experiment a little more with a phrase or a word. With practice I'm confident you'll find something that can return you to a more comfortable state. When you reach that emotional state, where you're comfortable enough, you can move on to step two.

Step Two: Circle back.

Sometimes it will be obvious that you've made a mistake as you try to support your person, but other times it won't be. Sometimes you'll just feel weird and wonder if anyone else noticed. If you know that your mistake was harmful, you can jump straight to Step Three. But if you're unclear, circle back with your person. Dig deep into your courage bucket and ask a simple question like:

> *Hey, I've been feeling weird about [our last conversation/what happened this morning/etc.]. When I said/did/acted [...]. Did that make you feel uncomfortable?*

If you've been following the steps in this book, you'll have empowered your person to be honest with you. You've let them know that you will love them no matter what so they feel confident sharing feedback with you. If you haven't shared that you love them unconditionally yet, you'll want to share that affirmation before circling back for feedback on the specific event or conversation.

Remain open to what your person shares about how your words or actions were perceived. I know it's difficult to hear when you haven't done something right, but being able to listen and alter your behavior for the future will ultimately make you a better grief ally for your person—not to mention, a better friend.

Step Three: Apologize to your person (if necessary).

If the mistake that you've made was hurtful to your person, dismissive, invalidating, damaging, or anything less than helpful, then the best thing you can do is apologize. That said, it's important to know that not all apologies are created equal.

In *When Sorry Isn't Enough: Making Things Right with Those You Love*, co-authors Jennifer Thomas, a psychologist and apology critic, and Gary Chapman, the creator of the five love languages, identify five apology languages.[35] These five languages make up the fundamental aspects of an apology. Each one is important, but based on their research, Chapman and Thomas have discovered that different people value different aspects of an apology based on their preferred apology language. Similar to understanding Chapman's five languages of love, when you know someone's preferred apology language, you're making it easier for them to genuinely forgive you because you've demonstrated your remorse and sincerity in a way that they uniquely comprehend.

If you have the time and want to improve your apology skills, I would recommend using *When Sorry Isn't Enough* as your starting point, but if you don't have that kind of time, here are a few quick tips for making an effective apology:

- Always be as specific as possible. Identify the exact

language, behavior, or choice that you are remorseful for.

- Never use the word "but" in an apology. Apologies with a "but" in them are excuses not apologies.
- Do not use apologies to manipulate your person into getting what you want from them.[36]

Then, after you've made your apology, you need to patiently wait for your person to accept it. That's the fourth and final step.

Step Four: Let your apology breathe.

The next step isn't about doing anything per se. Rather, this step is about giving your person time to feel whatever it is they need to feel and are allowed to feel about what you've done. Being patient after delivering an apology is probably the most difficult step after you've found the courage to ask for feedback and accept responsibility for your actions. But giving your person some time to absorb your remorse is critical. In their book, Chapman and Thomas make the following plea:

> "Please understand that when you request to be forgiven, you are making a huge request. It will be costly to the person you have offended. When they forgive you, they must give up their desire for justice. They must relinquish their hurt and anger, their feeling of embarrassment or humiliation. They must give up their feelings of rejection and betrayal. Sometimes, they must live with the consequences of your wrong behavior."[37]

You'll be asking your person to release all of those conditions on top of grieving the death of their beloved, which is also stacked on top of all of the change that is being created because of that death. That is a lot of energy being expended. So, please be as kind and as patient as you can be after you've delivered an apology.

The good news here, though, is that despite the fact that apologizing and waiting for your person to fully accept your apology might be excruciating, if it's done properly, you'll actually be strengthening the relationship you have with your person.

How Person-Ships Get Stronger

Will was the most gorgeous man I'd ever had the pleasure of spending time with. He was generous, kind, and thoughtful, but my oh my! his body was wonderful too. For the first three months that we were together, my friends and I affectionately referred to him as 0%, which was short for 0% body fat. The secret nickname was obviously an exaggeration because having no body fat is impossible and striving for it is unhealthy in a number of ways, but Will was beyond dedicated to his gym regime and it showed.

In the hard times we spent together, Will would remind me that muscles are not built in the gym but rather they are broken down there. Pushing, pulling, and struggling to lift all of that heavy stuff at the gym creates tiny tears in the muscles. What actually builds muscle and makes them stronger is proper rest and recovery after all that damage has been done. He lived by the notion that we don't get stronger or faster or better at whatever we're trying to do unless we recover with as much intention as we had when we worked out. He believed that struggle is what strengthened the relationships between people and brought them together. After Will's death, I know this is true too.

The relationships that exist between me and those people who have shown up for me since Will died and in the ways that I have needed them to show up—my front row—have only gotten stronger. That outcome has been especially true when these loved ones have been vulnerable enough for me to give them feedback when I've felt like their words or actions missed their mark. Like a muscle that's been worked and broken down through struggle, those relationships have been strengthened with vulnerability, courage, and time to properly recover.

The connection that exists between you and your person is a muscle composed of trust, love, and respect. That connection will only deepen if you are willing to be courageous and make mistakes to be there for them as they learn how to exist in the world without their beloved. That muscle is what you can return to over and over as you and your person journey through the long haul of their grief—even when you think your person might need more support than you and the rest of their front row can offer.

Comfort and Ease: Ideas for How to Be a Grief Ally

- **Know your person's love language.**

    Gary Chapman's five languages of love are the gold standard for any kind of person-ship goals.[38] Knowing your person's love language can help you express that you really do love your person unconditionally and that you're willing to keep showing up despite the fact that you will make some mistakes.

- **Try to figure out your person's preferred apology language.**

    There are several articles online about the five apology languages that Thomas and Chapman have defined in *When Sorry Isn't Enough*. Go exploring and learn more about each of these five languages. That way, when you need to make an apology, you'll be more equipped to offer one that is specific and meaningful to your person.

- **Here are a few gift ideas:**

    I'm not suggesting that for every mistake that you make you need to offer a gift to recover, or that if your person's love language speaks to gifts, then you need to spend oodles of dollars on them. But…if you are making a shopping list, make sure you're using the principles of comfort and ease to create it. Here are two things that I believe are mandatory for anyone living with the loss of a beloved:

    - **A weighted blanket**

        There's some science that says weighted blankets are great for helping with anxiety or insomnia. To be honest, I just love my weighted blanket because it feels like I'm being held. It's a great tool to have on hand when a hug is what your person could use, but they don't have someone present to offer one.

- **A long coat or sweater**

    When grieving, it's not uncommon to skip showering, to wear the same clothes for days, or spill stuff down the front of a shirt and not have the energy to put on a clean one. Appearance shouldn't be something that your person has to worry about. Having a long coat or sweater with a collar that reaches their chin and falls at or below their knees is a tool that I recommend having on hand. With this cover-up, they can throw it on and leave the house without having to worry about what's underneath.

CHAPTER 8

THE LONG HAUL AND BEYOND

I promise to follow the steps and keep my promises.

What Doing the Wrong Thing Really Looks Like

In 2017, Kelly Lynn, a comedian, author, and a widow, gave a Tedx Talk called "When Someone You Love Dies, There's No Such Thing as Moving On."[39] Since then, it has earned over two million views on YouTube (hopefully more since the publishing of this book). In her talk, Kelly tells the story of a widow who goes to the cemetery all the time to visit her husband. She keeps a lawn chair in the trunk of her car so she can sit with him at his graveside. One day, this widow went out to her car and found that her chair was gone. Two friends took responsibility for the missing chair, admitting that they took it away because they didn't think it was healthy for her to go to the cemetery anymore. They thought it would be better for her to move on.

This is not grief allyship.

It was probably quite difficult for these two friends to watch someone they care about miss her husband so intensely and with such frequency, but instead of being willing to sit with their own discomfort they took it upon themselves to problem-solve. Instead of offering reverence to their widowed friend and her grief, they concluded that if she no longer spent time at her dead husband's grave then she would be better off. She would stop grieving. Their intention was not the right thing to do. These friends didn't help their friend. They helped themselves. They wanted her to get better and to stop grieving for their own comfort.

Their actions didn't help their friend at all. Instead, they sent the message that their friend's grief was no longer welcome with them. Their actions didn't put an end to this woman's grief. She didn't stop missing her husband. She didn't stop wanting to be near him. That widow still goes to the cemetery, but now she goes in secret. She also has two fewer friends who are unsafe to share her truest self with.

Determining whether someone is grieving in a "healthy way" is a complex task that should be left to a professional. Grief never ends. Still expressing grief years after someone has died isn't wrong or unhealthy. Just because you can't see someone's grief doesn't mean it's not there. So, in this chapter I'm going to give you some guidance about when to know if your person needs extra support and point out the value of following the steps that I've laid out in helping them survive the death of their beloved because I know you love them and you want them to survive this.

When to Ask for More Help

> If you believe that your person is going to harm themselves, put down this book and call 911 or reach out to a local or national crisis line. Help is always available where there is internet access or telephone reception.

If you are concerned about your person and how they are grieving, that's okay. It means you care deeply about their well-being. But before you take action when you believe your person is grieving in an *unhealthy* way, ask yourself why you believe that? Where's the judgment coming from? Something someone told you? What you've witnessed in someone else's experience with grief? A movie you watched? A story you heard?

How grief is expressed and experienced can look a lot like the subtle warning signs associated with self-harm. Personally, I've experienced *all* of the subtle warning signs identified by Crisis Service Canada: feelings of helplessness or hopelessness; no sense of purpose in life; increased substance use; anxiety, agitation or uncontrolled anger; unable to sleep or sleeping all of the time; feelings of being trapped—like there's no way out; withdrawal from friends, family, and society; acting recklessly or engaging in risky activities seemingly without thinking; and dramatic mood changes. Hell, I've even experienced one of the most direct warning signs too: I talk about death—like a lot—and made comments about not wanting to be alive. But that doesn't mean I've ever wanted to be dead.

If your person isn't clearly expressing a desire or plan to harm themselves, it might be hard to determine if and when to intervene. The best tools you have for assessment are observation, your team, and your voice. Watch for signs that suggest your person is managing their grief in ways that are compromising their safety. Listen for threats or plans they're making to hurt themselves. Ask your person's team to do the same. You can also reach out for help and advice on your own. Crisis lines are resources for allies too, and they have skilled individuals who can help if you believe your person is in danger. And then, if it's time to intervene, use the love and empathy that you have for your person and put your worry into words. Ask directly: Are you thinking about hurting yourself? Or say: I think you need more help.

It will not be an easy conversation to have but please don't fear having it if you think it's necessary. Research suggests talking about suicide doesn't increase the likelihood that someone will harm themselves. In fact, connecting with someone who cares can decrease suicidal ideation.[40] Don't ignore the signs. Trust your judgment.

Talking about suicide doesn't increase the likelihood that someone will harm themselves. In fact, connecting with someone who cares can decrease suicidal ideation.

If you think that your person needs help from a professional team, the National Alliance on Mental Illness (NAMI) suggests these steps when having the tough conversation:

- Ensure your person knows that you will support them through the process of seeking professional support. They might be aware that they need help, but they could be afraid to seek it out if they're concerned about judgment or being treated differently by you.

- Be sensitive about where you have the conversation. Don't hold an intervention like you've seen on TV or in a public setting. As much as you can, keep the conversation private, compassionate, and relaxed.

- Prepare for resistance. Not everyone is open to professional help. You might need to be prepared to state your case if your person becomes defensive.
- Offer to help them find the support they need and want. Seeking help can be overwhelming and scary. You can help by accompanying them to their appointments and waiting in the car, or by making phone calls and helping them find the right kind of support.[41]

Whether or not your person needs extra support doesn't mean that there is anything wrong with them or with their grief. They are not less of a person. They have not failed. They are not weak. Every human is unique, so all grief is unique. Getting extra support just means that someone needs some extra support.

In an *Atlantic* article by Andrea Volpe entitled "Is Grief a Disease?" Donna Schuurman from the Dougy Center, which supports grieving children and families, was quoted saying, "Medicalizing or pathologizing the experience of someone who is having difficulty after a death does not do justice to the full social and cultural context in which he or she is grieving... Grief is not a medical disease, it is a human response to loss. Many people who are experiencing severe challenges after a loss are doing so because the social expectations around them are not supporting them."[42]

With this book, it is my hope that your person will get the social support that they need to survive the death of their beloved and reach a new kind of *okay-ish* at some point. Studies have shown that social support—anything that leads someone to believe that they are important, loved, cared for, and a member of a community—is a protective factor in suicide, as well as being critical to mental health, trauma recovery, and enduring the death of a loved one.[43] You can give your person that kind of social support by following the steps and keeping the promises I've laid out in this book.

Follow the Steps, Keep Your Promises

It's easy to drop a lasagna at someone's door and leave a card that says, "I'm here if you need me. Just call." It is not easy to follow the steps in this book because they require vulnerability, humility, and courage, but that's what your person needs.

If you can't follow the steps, you're putting the relationship you have with your person at risk. Do you want to lose them? Or are you willing to sacrifice your comfort to learn how to be the best support you can be for them to be able to live with their grief? I want you to be the kind of person who shows up for your friend no matter what. If you aren't committed to learning what grief is like for them, or how to listen without problem-solving, or having the courage to ask what they need and to make mistakes, you're not going to be able to offer the kind support that your person needs.

If you're not committed to this work, you're going to harm your person more than you will help them. You run the risk of pushing them away or losing a friend because you're not capable of giving them the kind of love that they need and deserve when bad things happen. You're going to regret losing them for that reason. I don't want you to live with regret.

I want you to have your person in your life for a long time. I want you to reach a new level of love, pride, and devotion for one another because of what you've helped each other live through. Friends who choose not to follow the steps and keep their promises don't get there.

As you follow the steps and keep your promises, the relationship between you and your person will get stronger. Over time you'll reach a new equilibrium. A new dynamic will develop between the two of you that honors what you've both learned and experienced because of the death of their beloved. That's what happens when you follow the steps and keep your promises.

These steps and promises are something you can apply every time another event happens in your person-ship—another loss, weddings, babies, big mistakes, etc. After Will died, in the lives of my front-row group there were a number of babies born and two significant weddings happened. Do you know what my community did? Yes, they followed the steps and kept their promises.

- Take good care of yourself.
- Let your person be the expert of their grief.
- Support the rest of their team.
- Listen actively.
- Skip clichés, ask questions, and tell the truth.
- Have the courage to keep showing up when you make mistakes.
- Ask for more help if you need it.

Love Isn't Always Comfortable

Love is both a verb and a noun. Either way, love must be active in order to be true. Erich Fromm, a psychoanalyst and social philosopher, argues that love is an art, and like any other kind of art it takes humility, courage, faith, and discipline to experience real love.[44] The foundation of grief allyship is unconditional love, the kind that we all deserve as human beings.

Loving your person through the long haul of their grief will not be comfortable. Being in a learning environment isn't an easy place to be in for a long period of time. At some points, you might wish that you could just download the software and be ready to go because learning is exhausting. But please stick with it. Have the courage and discipline to stay close even when things are uncomfortable. Have the faith that the love you and your person have between you is worth showing up for.

Your person deserves to be loved through their most painful moments. I hate that I have to write that line down. But the reality is that not everyone is accepted and loved as they are while they're doing their best to reconcile a heartbreak. Because of that negligence, we have a culture that doesn't understand grief. That culture has left the bereaved to support one another in isolation. Your person deserves better than that. You can help them have a better future than those who have come before them.

Comfort and Ease: Ideas for How to Be a Grief Ally

- **Have preparatory conversations before big events.**

    If you and your person are going to a big event that has the potential to be triggering for them—wedding, baby shower, family reunion, funeral, etc.—have a conversation to (1) acknowledge that it might be difficult, (2) reiterate that your person is the expert in what they need and that they are allowed to do whatever they want to do to endure this event, including not attending, (3) make a plan to get whatever special accommodations they might need (i.e., to know where they can go if they need to be alone, to know the steps to bringing their therapy dog, whether they want a memorial seat for their beloved, or do they not want their beloved mentioned at all, etc., and (4) let them know they will be loved no matter how or if they show up to this event.

- **Offer to take the lead when you can.**

    Living in grief takes a lot of energy to ensure that you are getting what you need—from the basics (food, water, shelter) to exercising your leadership muscles so that others will exist around you in a way that feels the best. All of that effort is exhausting. When you can, offer to take the lead in situations with your person. Can you make the plans or reservations? Can you suggest the place to meet? Can you decide on the menu with confidence? Can you ask what their non-negotiables are and take the planning from there? That'll make your person's life easier.

- **Acknowledge all of their losses.**

  Your person has not only lost their beloved. There are a number of things that your person will not be able to do, have, and be because their beloved has died. As they move forward over time, do not forget that they will grieve these losses as well. Acknowledging how things are different than what they were supposed to be or should be can provide a lot of comfort.

CHAPTER 9

WELCOME TO THE GRIEF REVOLUTION

Will died when he was 29; I was 30. One of the most heartbreaking realities that I've had to face since his death is that I might live for 50 or more years without him. As the physical symptoms of my grief have become more manageable and as more time passes since Will's death, I worry a lot about the future.

I fear the looks that I might have to endure in 5, 10, or 25 years from now when I tell stories about how much it hurts to live in a world without Will. I'm afraid of my grief being dismissed when he will have been dead longer than we got to be together. I'm afraid of meeting new people and having them ask if I'm single. *Well, kind of, yes. But not really, no.* And then having to explain why it's so difficult for me to answer that question. I worry that one day people will stop talking about Will. I want him, I need him, to be in my life forever. I know that with my leadership that he will be, but having people around me who are willing to help me do that will make my life so much easier.

I wrote this book because I'm one of the people who needs

this book. People who have suffered a great loss need to believe that there's a future for us where our lives can still be big and full and that our grief can exist within it. We can't have that future if the people around us aren't willing to be there for us through the long haul of grief. Your person can't have that kind of future without your help.

By reading this book and taking the steps I've laid out to help support your grieving person, you're giving them the best chance at living a full life where they get to be their truest self. Everyone deserves to be able to show up in the world and be seen as the whole human beings that we are. After all, death is guaranteed for everyone. Everyone at some point in their lives will experience grief. This fundamental human experience shouldn't be covered up and hidden behind closed doors. But it takes courage and energy to change the status quo, both of which are in short supply early in our grief and why we, your person and people like me—survivors of the grief earthquakes—need help from people like you.

The Future Needs to Be Different

When a beloved dies, those who are left behind are likely (or will be) bombarded with messages of "Find community!" and "Find people like you. They can help!" But because of the uninformed way our culture has treated the bereaved for some time now, I'm not surprised that it's become the "thing to do" after the death of someone that you love.

It takes a lot of courage for those who have not lived through the life-shattering experience of loss to hold space for those who have. Not everyone has that kind of courage, but you've gotten this far, so I know that you do. That's why the grief revolution needs you.

The people who don't have your kind of courage are not capable of sitting with one in mourning as they painfully learn to live in a world without their children, spouse, parent, sibling, best friend, etc. Many will, knowingly or unknowingly, encourage their loved ones to suppress or hide their grief. Messages like "maybe it's time for you to move on" or "you have to make a choice to either sink or swim" or "*at least* you got five good years with him (...so stop feeling so bad)" or outright silence will send a clear message to your person. That message is *you're making me uncomfortable, so hurry up and get over this, please, so we can get back to the life we had before you were grieving.*

This kind of treatment has created a culture-wide suppression of grief. That is a problem because it encourages those of us who have lost a loved one to tell others that we're "fine" and to endure our grief behind closed doors, entirely alone or with only a select few who won't hurry us through what's uncomfortable. When we're out in the world, we'll fake it. We'll swallow the sadness to blend in with the people who are oblivious to what grief feels like. We push it down and dress it up with our best fake smiles so that those whom we are with will think that we're "fixed" because there is a risk in every interaction that they won't be able to hold space for our discomfort and that if we share our truth, we'll be dismissed or avoided completely.

We don't talk about our grief because our culture makes it not safe to talk about it. All those lasagnas at the doorstep followed by the fake *I'm fine*'s perpetuate a cycle of naive and ultimately unhelpful grief support.

When I read the stories of people willing to share their experiences of living with grief, it worries me. Hope Edelman was 17 when her mother died. Nearly 40 years after her mother's death, Edelman published *The AfterGrief*, a book about the long arc of loss. In the introduction, she talks about how it has been 39 years since her mother died:

> "*Thirty nine years and you're not over it yet?*
>
> "Anyone with major loss in the past knows this question well. We've spent years fielding versions of it, explicit and implied, from parents, siblings, spouses, partners, relatives, colleagues, acquaintances, and friends. We recognize the subtle cues - the slight eyebrow lift, the soft, startled "Oh! That *long* ago? - from those who wonder how an event so distant can still occupy such precious mental and emotional real estate. Why certain, specific nodes are still so tender when poked.
>
> "How many of us have wondered the same?
>
> "*You're* still *not over it yet*? As if the death of a loved one were a hurdle in a track meet that could be cleared and left behind."[45]

We don't get over our grief. We don't move on. Our grief doesn't get fixed. It doesn't go away. If your person wants a life where the truth of their grief can be openly expressed, their world could become much smaller because not everyone is like you and capable of accepting the truth about grief. I don't want that scenario for your person. Selfishly, I don't want it for myself either. But as I've listened to the stories of people who have lost their loved ones before me, it's clear that for some of us, it begins to feel like that might be the safest option.

The subtle cues Edelman references are harmful and discouraging, putting anyone who is bereaved at risk for internalizing some level of shame…shame for not being able to leave their beloved, someone they'd never choose to live without, in the past. Shame is painful, and it happens when we're burned for being vulnerable. Hilary Jacobs Hendel writes,

> "The mind of someone who has been burned more than once for exposing her authentic Self might say, *Let's just keep our Self as small and hidden as possible, so no one can hurt us. If we expand and reach out into the world to discover new things, we will get slammed down again. Play it safe by staying small and hidden away.* And so we do."[46]

I refuse to believe that mindset is the way the future has to be for your person, but the bereaved cannot change the future on their—*our*—own. To live the biggest lives that we can, the bereaved need to be able to carry forward the memory of those we've lost. I want a future where the paradox of being human is welcomed out in the open and where we acknowledge the reality that when someone we love dies, we'll always miss them. And although that reality is sad and uncomfortable, it gets to live alongside all the good things that happen in life too. Your allyship will make that future come true.

Your Allyship Is Revolutionary

In the simplest of ways, you are already part of this grief revolution. Your willingness to learn what you can do to support your person rather than rely on clichés and casseroles is a revolutionary act. Your willingness to make mistakes and keep showing up is a revolutionary act. Your commitment to just reading this book is a revolutionary act.

The status quo will begin to change when the voices of those who have experienced the cruelest reality of being human are amplified and echoed by allies like you. A good illustration of that outcome comes from my own life through an unexpected conversation I had with my mom.

One afternoon, Mom and I were chatting via text message. I was feeling particularly cheeky that day, so when my mom wrote, "I hope you don't mind, but there are a few women at work who ask about you and wonder how you're doing." I snapped back with, "I hope you don't tell them I'm fine." In the kind and eager tone that my mom is known for, she responded with, "No, I tell them that every day is hard for you and it probably will be for some time." How revolutionary!

My mom being a leader in her own circles about how grief doesn't get resolved is a great example of how we change the culture of grief—one person at a time. When people ask her how I'm doing she doesn't say "she's fine." Instead, she shares that every day is hard, that I struggle to find the desire to exist in this world without Will, and that I live with a heartbreaking void every day.

That simple answer from my mom to her work colleagues is revolutionary and is the last step in your work as a grief ally. When you've finished this book, as you sit in the front row of your person's classroom, learning how to do better at grief support than many will ever be, be willing to share what you learn with others. To be clear, I'm not suggesting that you share the intimate details of your person's experience, but rather the lessons you've learned by sitting with your person in their pain. That's where the seeds of change are cultivated. By sharing with others about what grief is really like, how it doesn't disappear, how it can't be fixed, and how it can change a person will begin to change how everyone understands grief—not exclusively the grievers and their allies. This expansion of knowing will help your person, and so many others like them, have a life that is big and full and overflowing with love and belonging. That's the end game for a grief ally.

You Will Never Be Alone as a Grief Ally

There are so many people in the world like you who want to help the people they love after the loss of a loved one. There are plenty of great resources out there to help you find real-life lessons from people experiencing grief. I also recommend Kelly Lynn's Ted Talk "When Someone You Love Dies, There Is No Such Thing as Moving On," and Megan Devine's book, *It's OK That You're Not OK*. I've also created a master resource list that you can find at the end of this book with my recommendations for additional books, podcasts, talks, and online platforms to check out.

I'm also available to help you. If you want to dive deeper into grief allyship, sort through some of the challenges you're experiencing, or need a safe space to express your own grief, I would be happy to help. As a life coach, I can help you with the following:

- Finding the motivation and courage you need to show up, have hard conversations, and witness hard things despite being afraid
- Giving you a safe space to express your frustration and anger because you can't fix your person's grief
- Creating your own unique strategy for taking care of yourself
- Actively listening to your own experience of grief because of the changes you're witnessing in your person

- Helping to get you off the shame rollercoaster when you've accidentally made mistakes
- Giving you guidance when you're at a loss for what to do next to be helpful to your person

I also offer Grief Allyship training workshops for small to large groups, and I'm available as a speaker. You can learn more about my current offerings and watch for upcoming events on my website www.alybird.com, or you can find me on social media @thealybird. If you follow me, say hello. I'd love to hear from you.

You're Already Doing a Good Job

When someone dies, the world around you—not just the world around your person—can become chaotic and overwhelming. When my friend Sarah was on a seven-hour journey to get to me after Will had died, she told me that she got stuck on the same page of Elizabeth Gilbert's novel *City of Girls* for the entire flight. She read the same 400 words over and over again because her brain wasn't able to take them in. Finishing this book amidst the disarray in your life right now might have seemed nearly impossible. And yet, you've done it.

This relatively invisible act shows how fiercely you love your person, and it gives me so much hope for the future: one where people who have to live with the most painful reality of being human are loved and cared for just as they are, grief and all. Those who have known such a great loss deserve a future where they are surrounded by people who will not shy away from their pain, but stand next to them and fight for them to continue to have big lives full of love, understanding, and belonging. From the depths of my being, thank you. Thank you for being a part of this grief revolution, and thank you for your allyship.

MY MASTER RESOURCE LIST

As promised, here are the resources that I specifically recommend when you're looking to learn more about grief.

Books

It's OK That You're Not OK: Meeting Grief and Loss in a Culture that Doesn't Understand by Megan Devine

The AfterGrief: Finding Your Way Along the Long Arc of Loss by Hope Edelman

Organizations and Online Platforms

being here, human

Modern Loss

Speaking Grief

Refuge in Grief

What's Your Grief

Podcasts

Grief is a Sneaky B!tch by Lisa Keefauver

Grief Out Loud by The Dougy Center

Here After with Megan Devine

Stories about Death, Dying, and Grief

Bearing the Unbearable: Love, Loss, and the Heartbreaking Path of Grief by Joanne Cacciatore

Modern Loss: Candid Conversation about Grief. Beginners Welcome. by Rebecca Soffer, Gabrielle Birkner

Radical Acts of Love: Twenty Conversations to Inspire Hope at the End of Life by Janie Brown

"The Love of My Life" by Cheryl Strayed

Talks

"We don't 'move on' from grief, we move forward" by Nora McInerny

"When Someone You Love Dies, There Is No Such Thing as Moving On" by Kelly Lynn

Articles

Dual Process Model of Coping with Bereavement: Rational and Description by Margaret Stroebe and Henk Schut, *Death Studies*, 1993

How Not to Say the Wrong Thing by Susan Silk and Barry Goldman, *LA Times*, 2013

ACKNOWLEDGEMENTS

This book would not be possible without the following people:

My family, who always believes in my brain and what it can accomplish.

Sarah, I always thought of myself as Cristina, and not Meredith, but you have been the best Cristina ever. Thank you to you and Katelyn for being my chosen sisters.

To my Home Team, thank you for always being in my corner.

Mallory, Chris, Bodi, and Rupert, thank you for being my second home.

Michelle, your words will bring me comfort, over and over and over again.

Martin, the strength of your hugs has surprised me. Thank you for humoring me and my dedication to Tom Hardy.

Lauren and Mike, thank you for your home, taking me to The Dime, and never missing an opportunity to visit The Whistle Stop.

Katie, you light up my heart with your love for dancing, dessert, and DIY gifts.

Kara and Terry, you are the kindest and most generous friends and neighbors.

Jen and kiddos, you are all the coolest. Thank you for taking care of me.

Zeneta and Sloan, you probably never worked harder than you did with my family. Thank you for doing it with such kindness, patience, and compassion.

Tamara, Saskia, and Alex, I am so grateful for what you've taught me about how to take care of myself in ways that I never would have learned on my own.

Julia, thank you for being this book's fairy godmother.

To the rest of my front row, I would not be this far on the other side of the moment that changed my life forever if it wasn't for your allyship. I am so grateful.

Special thank you's go out to: Ally Fallon, Annie, and Ashley at Find Your Voice for giving regular ol' people a space to believe in the stories they want to tell; to Steph Jagger and her flight of birds who continue to check in and believe in me; to Megan Devine and the Writing Your Grief alumni community who have taught me how to be an ally; to everyone who supported the Go Fund Me Campaign that helped me be with the people who gave me the greatest comfort after Will died; to Sochi who sat with me while this idea transformed into a book; and to Renegade who came along halfway through and ensured that I took the breaks that I needed.

A noteworthy mention is necessary for Taylor Swift and her complete discography that will keep me company through any emotion for the rest of my life. Taylor, if you're reading this, I love you.

ENDNOTES

1. Joanne Cacciatore et al., "What is good grief support? Exploring the actors and actions in social support after traumatic grief," *PLOS One* 16, no. 5 (May 27, 2021), https://www.doi.org/10.1371/journal.pone.0252324.

2. Julia Samuels, *Grief Works: Stories of Life, Death and Surviving* (New York: Penguin, 2017). p.255

3. John Bowlby, *Attachment: Attachment and Loss*, vol. 1 (New York: Basic Books, 1983).

4. John Bowlby, *Attachment: Attachment and Loss*, vol. 3 (New York: Pimlico, 1998).

5. Kenneth J. Doka and Terry L. Martin, *Grieving Beyond Gender: Understanding the Ways Men and Women Mourn* (Milton Park, UK: Routledge, 2010), 18.

6. The famous *On Grief and Grieving: Finding the Meaning of Grief Through the Five Stages of Loss* book by Elizabeth Kübler-Ross and David Kessler was published in 2005. They took lessons learned from patients dying of terminal illnesses, the work published in Kübler-Ross' *On Death and Dying* (1969), and applied it to people living with grief.

7. Doka and Martin, *Grieving Beyond Gender*, ix.

8. Ibid., 55.

9. *The AfterGrief*, Hope Edelman The AfterGrief, accessed June 23, 2022, https://theaftergrief.com.

10. Robert M. Sapolsky, *Why Zebras Don't Get Ulcers: The Acclaimed Guide to Stress, Stress-Related Diseases, and Coping* (New York: Henry Holt and Company, 2004).

11. Hilary Jacobs Hendel, *It's Not Always Depression: Working the Change Triangle to Listen to the Body, Discover Core Emotions, and Connect to Your Authentic Self* (New York: Random House, 2018), 4.

12. Susan Silk and Barry Goldman, "How not to say the wrong thing," the *Los Angeles Times*, April 7, 2013, https://www.latimes.com/opinion/op-ed/la-xpm-2013-apr-07-la-oe-0407-silk-ring-theory-20130407-story.html.

13. Ibid.

14. Alan D. Wolfelt, *Companioning the Bereaved: A Soulful Guide for Counselors & Caregivers* (Fort Collins, CO: Companion Press, 2005).

15. Abby Wambach, *WOLFPACK: How to Come Together, Unleash Our Power, and Change the Game* (New York: Celadon Books, 2019), 36.

16. Ibid., 39.

17. Bessel Van Der Kolk, *The Body Keeps the Score: Brain, Mind, and Body in the Healing of Trauma* (New York: Penguin, 2015), 55.

18. Kübler-Ross and Kessler, *On Grief and Grieving*, 63.

19. Hendel, *It's Not Always Depression*, 95.

20. Van Der Kolk, *The Body Keeps the Score*, 81.

21 Devine, *It's OK That You're Not OK*, 21.

22 Graham D. Bodie et al., "The Role of 'Active Listening' in Informal Helpful Conversations: Impact on Perceptions of Listener Helpfulness, Sensitivity, and Supportiveness and Discloser Emotional Improvement," *Western Journal of Communication* 79, no. 2 (January 2015): 151–173, https://www.doi.org/10.1080/10570314.2014.943429.

23 Namkje Koudenburg et al., "Resounding Silences: Subtle Norm Regulation in Everyday Interactions," *Social Psychology Quarterly* 76, no. 3 (September 2013): 224–241, https://doi.org/10.1177/0190272513496794.

24 Brett Q. Ford et al., "The psychological health benefits of accepting negative emotions and thoughts: Laboratory, diary, and longitudinal evidence," *Journal of Personal Social Psychology* 115, no. 6 (December 2018): 1075–1092, https://www.doi.org/10.1037/pspp0000157.

25 "Stress won't go away? Maybe you are suffering from chronic stress," American Psychological Association, October 25, 2019, https://www.apa.org/topics/stress/chronic.

26 Hendel, *It's Not Always Depression*, 173

27 Doka and Martin, *Grieving Beyond Gender*, 65.

28 Devine, *It's OK That You're Not OK*, 20.

29 David Kessler, *Finding Meaning: The Sixth Stage of Grief* (Louisville, CO: Sounds True, 2017), 33.

30 Devine, *It's OK That You're Not OK*, 24.

31 George A. Bonnano, *The Other Side of Sadness: What the New Science of Bereavement Tells Us About Life After Loss* (New York: Basic Books, 2010), 106.

32 Stroebe, M, and H Schut, "The dual process model of coping with bereavement: rationale and description," *Death Studies* 23, no. 3 (1999): 197-224, https://www.doi.org/10.1080/074811899201046.

33 Hendel, *It's Not Always Depression*, 172.

34 Brené Brown, *Dare to Lead: Brave Work. Tough Conversations. Whole Hearts*, 78.

35 Gary Chapman and Jennifer Thomas, *When Sorry Isn't Enough: Making Things Right with Those You Love* (Chicago, IL: Moody Publishers, 2013).

36 Ibid.

37 Ibid., 118.

38 Gary Chapman, *The 5 Love Languages: The Secret to Love That Lasts* (Chicago, IL: Northfield Publishing, 2015).

39 Tedx Talks, "When Someone You Love Dies, There Is No Such Thing as Moving On | Kelley Lynn | TEDxAdelphiUniversity," YouTube video, May 5, 2017, https://www.youtube.com/watch?v=kYWlCGbbDGI.

40 Marina Murphy, "Does talking about suicide make someone more likely to commit suicide? Nevada Today, May 26, 2021, https://www.unr.edu/nevada-today/news/2021/atp-normalize-talking-about-suicide.

41 T. Dazzi et al., "Does asking about suicide and related behavior induce suicidal ideation? What is the evidence?" *Psychological Medicine* 44, no. 16 (December 2014): 3361-3, https://www.doi.org/10.1017/S0033291714001299.

42 Andrea Volpe, "Is Grief a Disease?" *The Atlantic*, November 16, 2016, https://www.theatlantic.com/health/archive/2016/11/

when-grief-never-ends/507752/.

43 Evan M. Kleiman et al., "Social support as a protective factor for suicide..." *Journal of Affective Disorders* 150, no. 2 (September 5, 2013): 54–545, https://www.doi.org/10.1016/j.jad.2013.01.033; Tayebeh Fasihi Harandi et al., "The correlation of social support with mental health: A meta-analysis," *Electronic Physician* 9, no. 9 (September 2017): 5212–5222, https://www.doi.org/10.19082/5212

44 Erich Fromm, *The Art of Loving* (New York: Harper Perennial, 2006), xiiii.

45 Edelman, *The AfterGrief*, xvi.

46 Hendel, *It's Not Always Depression*, 180.

CPSIA information can be obtained
at www.ICGtesting.com
Printed in the USA
JSHW051940301122
34125JS00002B/104